F4U CORSAIR
vs
Ki-84 "FRANK"
Pacific Theater 1945

EDWARD M. YOUNG

First published in Great Britain in 2016 by Osprey Publishing
PO Box 883, Oxford, OX1 9PL, UK
1385 Broadway, 5th Floor
New York, NY 10018

Osprey Publishing, part of Bloomsbury Publishing Plc

E-mail: info@ospreypublishing.com

A CIP catalog record for this book is available from the British Library

ISBN: 978 1 4728 1460 9
PDF ISBN: 978 1 4728 1461 6
ePub ISBN: 978 1 4728 1462 3

Edited by Tony Holmes
Cover artwork and battlescene by Gareth Hector
Three-views, cockpits, armament scrap views and Engaging the Enemy
artwork by Jim Laurier
Index by Mark Swift
Typeset in Adobe Garamond and Conduit ITC
Map and formation diagrams by Bounford.com
Originated by PDQ Media, Bungay UK
Printed in China through Worldprint Ltd

16 17 18 19 20 10 9 8 7 6 5 4 3 2 1

Osprey Publishing supports the Woodland Trust, the UK's leading woodland
conservation charity. Between 2014 and 2018 our donations will be spent on
their Centenary Woods project in the UK.

www.ospreypublishing.com

Previous Page

Capt Tadao Ikeda, CO of the 51st Sentai, stands by the tail of one of the
Ki-84s he flew during the war. Ikeda assumed command of the 51st in
December 1944 and remained with the unit until the end of the war. After
withdrawing from the Philippines, the Sentai reformed and flew Ki-84s in
defense of the Home Islands from Shimodate, northeast of Tokyo. (Dr. Yasuho
Izawa)

F4U Cover Art

Marine Air Group (MAG) 14 began re-equipping with the F4U-4 Corsair on
May 15, 1945 and on June 8 it arrived with its new airplanes on Okinawa.
MAG-14's three Corsair squadrons started flying combat air patrols (CAPs) the
next day. On June 21 a division from VMF-223 was flying a late CAP when the
division leader spotted a formation of 12 Japanese fighters flying in near line
abreast. Closing in on the formation, the pilots identified the Japanese fighters as
"Tojos," although they were more likely to have been "Franks" from the 26th
Shimbu-Tai unit, with an escort of more Ki-84s from the 47th Hikō Sentai.
Using the superior speed of their F4U-4s, 1Lt Martin Tiernan and his wingman,
1Lt John Groot, closed on a section flying on the right side of the formation.
Tiernan quickly shot down the wingman, hitting the Japanese fighter in the
cockpit. Another "Frank" then turned, attempting to get on Tiernan's tail. The
JAAF pilot opened fire as he closed on the Corsair, Tiernan seeing tracers flying
over his right wing. As he pulled up to evade his pursuer, Tiernan's wingman
came in on the "Frank" from above and behind and shot it down with two short
bursts. Both Ki-84s went down smoking and crashed into the sea below. (Cover
artwork by Gareth Hector)

Ki-84 Cover Art

On May 4, 1945, Maj Michiaki Tojo, commander of the 103rd Hikō Sentai, led
a formation of 30 Ki-84s from the 101st, 102nd and 103rd Hikō Sentai as
escorts for a mixed formation of Special Attack airplanes sent to attack US Navy
vessels off Okinawa. The Ki-84s had to zigzag above the slower bomb-laden
kamikaze. Near the island of Iheya Shima, northwest of Okinawa, the formation
spotted several American ships and the Special Attack airplanes began their final
dives. Flying above and monitoring the attack, Maj Tojo suddenly saw two F4U
Corsairs below him, intent on intercepting the Special Attack formation. One
Corsair turned to the right and came into firing range. Apparently unseen, Maj
Tojo opened fire and sent the F4U down smoking. The leading Corsair, probably
flown by Lt Saul Chernoff of VF-85, also turned to the right and failed to notice
the Ki-84s above until Maj Tojo was in a position to open fire, hitting Chernoff's
engine. The naval aviator dove away, with his Corsair smoking badly, and
successfully ditched. Chernoff was rescued, only to be killed subsequently on June
2, 1945 when VF-85 clashed with the N1K2-J "Georges" of the 343rd Kokutai
over Kyushu. (Cover artwork by Gareth Hector)

Acknowledgments

I would like to thank Ms. Naomi Williams for translating several articles on the
Type 4 Fighter and memories from former Hayate pilots. My good friend
Osamu Tagaya has again been generous with his time and extensive knowledge
of Japanese Army and Navy aviation in World War II. Jim Lansdale provided me
with copies of the Japanese Monograph Series relating to Home Defense.
Benjamin Kristy, Aviation Curator at the National Museum of the Marine
Corps, provided information on Capt William Snider of VMF-221. The images
for this volume came from Philip Jarrett, Dr. Yasuho Izawa, the National
Archives and Records Administration (NARA), the National Naval Aviation
Museum and the Museum of Flight in Seattle, Washington. I would like to
thank Holly Reed and her able staff at NARA, Hill Goodspeed and his
volunteers at the National Naval Aviation Museum and Amy Heidrick and
Jessica Jones at the Museum of Flight. P. J. Muller at the Museum of Flight
worked up the image to illustrate the problem of aircraft recognition. I would
also like to express my appreciation to artists Gareth Hector and Jim Laurier,
with whom I have worked on previous Osprey volumes. It has been a pleasure to
work with them again. Thanks to Tony Holmes at Osprey for his patience and
support of this and other projects. Lastly, I would like to express my appreciation
to my late father, who, as a young intelligence officer in a B-29 wing on Guam
in the summer of 1945, was responsible for tracking all sightings and
engagements with the Ki-84 "Frank." He sparked my interest in this exceptional
Japanese fighter airplane.

CONTENTS

INTRODUCTION

World War II was a conflict of industrial production on a massive scale. The Allies and the Axis powers converted their economies to unprecedented levels of war production, building aircraft, ships and weapons in prodigious quantities to cope with the demands of attrition in modern war. A significant proportion of this effort went to the production of airplanes. Concurrently, there was an equally significant emphasis on developing newer, more capable aircraft with improved speed, capacity, armament and protection to give a nation's pilots an advantage over their enemies in the battle for air superiority. Development was a never-ending process; if one side introduced a superior airplane, the other side had to develop an airplane that would at least meet, if not surpass, its capabilities. The duels between the Vought F4U Corsair and the Nakajima Type 4 Ki-84 Hayate (Gale) in the final months of the Pacific War were a product of this battle of development and production.

As described in *Osprey Duel 62 – F6F Hellcat vs A6M Zero-sen*, the American aviation industry was ahead of Japan in the development of high-powered air-cooled radial engines. Pratt & Whitney made the first test runs of its 18-cylinder R-2800 engine in 1939, initially at 1,800hp but with the potential for 2,000hp with further development. The Vought Corsair was the first American fighter airplane to be powered by the R-2800, and the first to exceed 400mph. For the US Navy, the Corsair represented a leap in performance over its first generation of monoplane carrier fighters, the Brewster F2A and the Grumman F4F. The Corsair was ruggedly built, with excellent speed, rate of roll and heavy armament of six 0.50-in machine guns. Its weaknesses – limited visibility over the nose on approach, poor stalling characteristics and directional instability on landing – initially made it unsuitable for carrier operations, but as a land-based fighter with the US Marine Corps in the Southwest Pacific it established a formidable reputation in battles against the vaunted Japanese Zero-sen.

Seeking a replacement for its Type 1 Fighter (the Nakajima Ki-43 Hayabusa), which entered service shortly before the start of the Pacific War, the Japanese Army Air Force (JAAF) turned to the Nakajima Aircraft Company to develop a successor. The JAAF was likely aware that the fighter would have to go up against this new second generation of American and British fighter airplanes, namely the Vought Corsair, Lockheed P-38 Lightning, Republic P-47 Thunderbolt and the latest models of the Supermarine Spitfire.

A group of US Marine Corps pilots from a squadron on Okinawa pose with an FG-1D behind them. "Marine Air" Corsair pilots had numerous encounters with the Ki-84 Hayate. (Record Group 127, GW-118645, NARA)

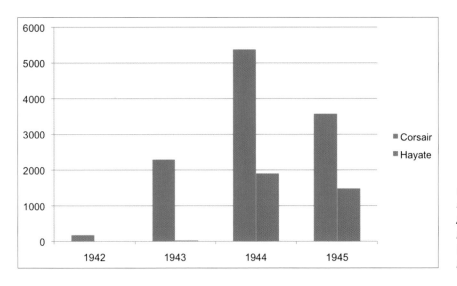

F4U and Ki-84 production 1942–45. [Sources – Dean, Francis H., *America's Hundred-Thousand: US Production Fighters of World War Two* and Wieliczko, Leszek A., *Nakajima Ki-84 Hayate*]

The Nakajima Type 4 Fighter Ki-84 Hayate ("Frank") went from design to combat in a little over two years. It combined a powerful engine with structural strength, heavier armament and better protection for the pilot and fuel. The Hayate was the JAAF's answer to the second generation of Allied fighter airplanes. (Peter M. Bowers Collection, Museum of Flight)

The JAAF also realized the need to combine the maneuverability of its "light" fighter aircraft like the Ki-43 with the more powerful armament of its "heavy" interceptor airplanes like the Nakajima Type 2 Shoki (Ki-44) in a fighter with superior performance and greater protection for the pilot, engine and fuel. Fortunately, Nakajima had begun working on its own 18-cylinder air-cooled radial engine, the Ha-45 Homare, that offered 1,800hp. This would power the company's Type 4 Fighter Ki-84 Hayate, an exceptional design incorporating superior performance that exceeded other JAAF fighters. It had more powerful armament, boasted outstanding maneuverability and had greater structural strength and armor protection. This was an airplane that could take on the best of Allied fighters. It is remarkable that the first flight of the Hayate took place only a little over a year after the JAAF approved Nakajima's design.

In designing a fighter airplane of the Hayate's caliber, the JAAF can be said to have won the development part of the battle. However, in the production battle, despite Herculean efforts, the JAAF fell well short. The Japanese aviation industry had no realistic hope of ever matching America's productive capacity. During the war Japan devoted an ever-greater amount of resources to aircraft production, doubling output during 1943 and nearly doubling it again during 1944. This was an impressive achievement, but during 1943 alone the American aviation industry built more airplanes than Japan did during the entire war.

The US Navy had the luxury of allocating production of the Corsair to two other companies besides Vought, the Brewster Aeronautical Corporation and the Goodyear Aircraft Company. Between them, they built three times as many Corsairs as Nakajima built Hayates. Production of the Ki-84 began to ramp up during 1944, just as the Japanese aviation industry reached its peak production levels and began an inexorable decline. The US Navy's submarine campaign against Japanese merchant shipping sharply reduced supplies of critical raw materials, especially the metals needed for high-powered airplane engines, leading to poorer quality engines and consequent maintenance problems. Although the Hayate was the most numerous JAAF fighter in the final months of the Pacific War, there were never enough to equip all of the JAAF's fighter regiments.

An F4U-1D from VF-84 prepares to launch on a mission from USS *Bunker Hill* (CV-17) on April 17, 1945. During the Okinawa campaign both US Navy and US Marine Corps Corsair squadrons flew from the large Essex-class fleet carriers. (RG80, 80-G-315378, NARA)

More critical to the outcome of duels between the Corsair and the Hayate was the poor quality of JAAF fighter pilots during the last year of the war. As fuel stocks declined, flying training was drastically curtailed. Indeed, by early 1945 JAAF pilots were receiving as little as 150 hours of flight training. While the Ki-84 was generally considered a straightforward aircraft for neophyte fighter pilots to fly, few had the experience needed to get the best out of their aircraft in combat with US Navy, US Marine Corps and US Army Air Force fighters. The appalling attrition of the air battles over the Philippines in late 1944 deprived the JAAF of hundreds of its more experienced fighter pilots.

The Corsair's higher speed, excellent acceleration and rate of roll gave US Navy and US Marine Corps pilots an advantage in combats with the Ki-84, but the lighter weight Hayate's superior maneuverability and rate of climb, coupled with its heavy armament, made the Nakajima fighter a dangerous opponent in the hands of an experienced pilot. In the air battles over the Japanese homeland and over Okinawa, well-trained US Navy and US Marine Corps Corsair pilots most often encountered Hayate pilots who were not up to their level of experience, leading to one-sided victories in these encounters.

CHRONOLOGY

1938

February   US Navy's Bureau of Aeronautics issues a tender for a new carrier fighter with performance superior to the XF2A-1 and XF4F-2.

June   Bureau of Aeronautics awards a contract to the Chance Vought Company for a prototype of the XF4U-1 with the new Pratt & Whitney XR-2800 engine.

1940

May 29   Lyman Bullard makes the first flight in the XF4U.

October   The XF4U-1 becomes the first US fighter airplane to exceed 400mph in level flight.

1941

June   The Bureau of Aeronautics gives Chance Vought a contract for 584 F4U-1 airplanes, named Corsair.

December   The Kōkū Hombu directs the Nakajima Company to begin work on a replacement for the Type 1 Fighter.

1942

May   The Kōkū Hombu approves the Nakajima design study for a new all-purpose fighter, which it designates the Ki-84.

June   First flight of the first production F4U-1.

September   Carrier qualification trials reveal serious deficiencies in landing characteristics of the F4U-1. The US Navy transfers the F4U to the US Marine Corps.

1943

February   The F4U-1 enters combat in the Southwest Pacific with VMF-124.

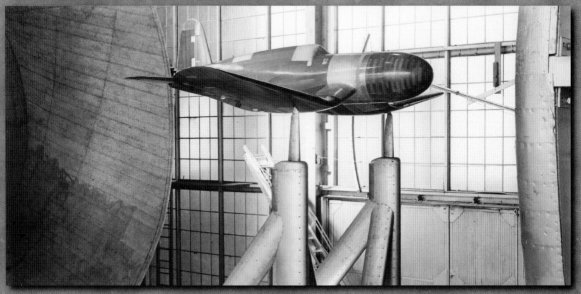

A wind tunnel model of the XF4U Corsair under test at the National Advisory Committee for Aeronautics facility at Langley, Virginia. (RG72-AC-25F-23, NARA)

F4U-1s under construction at the Vought factory in September 1943. In this month Vought and Goodyear Aircraft built 285 Corsairs. Production reached a peak in May 1944 when 596 Corsairs rolled out of the plants. (RG80, 80-G-150730, NARA)

April	First flight of the prototype Ki-84.
August	Second Ki-84 prototype completed, first pre-production aircraft ordered.

1944

January	Bureau of Aeronautics signs a contract with Chance Vought for 1,414 F4U-4 fighters.
March	22nd Hikō Sentai established as the first JAAF unit to receive the Ki-84 fighter.
April	First production Ki-84 completed as Type 4 Fighter Model 1 Hayate.
April	First flight of the XF4U-4 with Pratt & Whitney R-2800-18W engine.
August	The 22nd Hikō Sentai deploys to China with its Type 4 fighters.
September	First production F4U-4 delivered to the US Navy.
September	Carrier strikes on the Philippines begin.
October	Leyte invaded on October 24.

	Type 4 fighters heavily involved in combat over the Philippines, in China, and in Burma.
December	Following improvements in landing characteristics, the Corsair is approved for carrier duty. VMF-124 and VMF-213 assigned to USS *Essex* (CV-9).

1945

February	Carrier strikes on Tokyo bring the first combats between the Corsair and the Hayate.
April 1	Okinawa invaded, beginning intensive air combat in and around the island and the airfields on Kyushu and Honshu.
June 22	Okinawa declared secured. The JAAF decides to husband its strength for the coming invasion of Japan.
June–August	US Navy squadrons begin to re-equip with the F4U-4.

DESIGN AND DEVELOPMENT

VOUGHT F4U CORSAIR

In February 1938, with the Brewster XF2A and Grumman XF4F-2 then undergoing flight tests to determine which would be the US Navy's first monoplane carrier fighter, the Bureau of Aeronautics sent out a request to the American aviation industry for the next generation of carrier fighters with performance significantly in advance of the Brewster and Grumman prototypes. The Bureau wanted a fighter with a level speed of at least 350mph and armed with four machine guns, but with a low stalling speed of only 70mph for safe operation from carrier flightdecks.

Among the companies that responded was the Chance Vought Corporation, a subsidiary of the United Aircraft Corporation. A team under Vought's chief engineer Rex Beisel began working on two single-engined designs to meet the US Navy's request. In April 1938 Vought submitted its designs to the Bureau of Aeronautics. The V-166A featured the Pratt & Whitney R-1830 Twin Wasp engine of 1,000hp. The more ambitious design was the V-166B with the new Pratt & Whitney XR-2800 Double Wasp engine providing 1,850hp – the most powerful American air-cooled radial engine then available.

In June 1938, the Bureau of Aeronautics awarded a contract to Vought to build a prototype of its V-166B design as the XF4U-1. Rex Beisel and his team had created a

fighter that combined the most powerful air-cooled radial engine then available with a carefully streamlined design. To accommodate the large, 13ft diameter Hamilton Standard propeller needed to take advantage of the XR-2800's power, the design team came up with the ingenious solution of using an inverted gull wing, with the landing gear placed at the lowest point of the wing. The wing root sections attached to the fuselage accommodated the oil cooler for the engine and air inlets for the XR-2800 engine's two-stage supercharger.

The Vought XF4U-1 Corsair in April 1941. The prototype featured two 0.30in. machine guns in the nose firing through the huge Hamilton Standard propeller and a 0.50in. machine gun in each wing. (RG72, 72-AC-25C-14g, NARA)

The prototype XF4U-1 had two 0.30in. Browning AN/M2 machine guns in the nose firing through the propeller and one 0.50in. Browning M-2 machine gun in each wing. Small bomb-bays under each wing held fragmentation bombs, and a window beneath the pilot's seat gave him a view downward for dropping ordnance on formations of enemy bombers below. The forward position of the cockpit provided its occupant with good views over the inverted gull wing. Two fuel tanks in the wing center sections and two tanks in the outer wing held 273 gallons of fuel.

The XF4U-1 made its first flight on May 29, 1940, with Vought test pilot Lyman Bullard Jr at the controls. Bullard demonstrated the prototype to the Bureau of

Vought placed the cockpit of the XF4U-1 over the wings for better visibility. Early production models of the F4U-1 Corsair retained the "birdcage" canopy. (RG72, 72-AC-25C-14h, NARA)

The US Navy's decision to increase the Corsair's armament led to placing three 0.50in. machine guns in each wing. A fuselage fuel tank replaced the wing tanks, but moving the cockpit to the rear to accommodate the tank reduced visibility on takeoff and landing. (RG72, 72-AC-27A-102, NARA)

Aeronautics on October 1, 1940. During the demonstration the XF4U-1 attained a speed of 405mph, thus becoming the first American fighter airplane to surpass 400mph in level flight. After the Bureau of Aeronautics had conducted its own tests on the prototype, the US Navy awarded Vought a contract on June 30, 1941 for 541 F4U-1s. Choosing to assign names to its aircraft, the US Navy christened the new fighter the Corsair. With the increasing likelihood of war, and the need for substantial numbers of new fighter aircraft, the US Navy arranged for the F4U-1 to be built under license at the Brewster Aeronautical Corporation plant in Long Island as the F3A-1 and at the Goodyear Aircraft Plant in Akron, Ohio, as the FG-1.

With construction of the new Essex-class fleet carriers under way, and production of the F4U-1 beginning, the US Navy appeared well placed to have a new, powerful carrier fighter ready to serve on its new carriers. The only discordant note came from simulated carrier landings conducted in August 1941 where the prototype XF4U-1 demonstrated a disturbing tendency to drop the port wing suddenly when approaching stalling speed on landing.

Based on reports detailing aerial combat in Europe and the results of flight-testing, the Bureau of Aeronautics requested that Vought make a number of changes in the production version of the F4U-1. For example, its armament was enhanced to three 0.50in. machine guns in each outer wing in place of the nose-mounted 0.30in. weapons and the single 0.50in. wing guns, with substantially more ammunition totaling 2,350 rounds. The small wing bomb-bays were removed and the outer wing fuel tanks reduced in capacity. The fuel tanks in the wing center sections were also removed to accommodate the three 0.50in. machine guns and a much larger fuel tank installed in the fuselage between the engine and the cockpit. This required the fuselage to be lengthened by 17 inches and the cockpit to be moved 32 inches to the rear. More armor plate was fitted in and around the cockpit for greater protection of the pilot and the engine oil tank. The span of the ailerons was increased by 20 inches to improve the rate of roll.

An improvement in the performance of the Pratt & Whitney R-2800-8 engine, which now produced 2,000hp, ensured that the fighter's speed and rate of climb did not suffer from the additional weight of fuel, armor and armament. With the newer engine a production F4U-1 could attain a speed of 417mph at 20,000ft.

The first production aircraft emerged in June 1942, and three months later the seventh production airplane undertook carrier landing trials onboard USS *Sangamon* (CVE-26) in Chesapeake Bay. The trials were a disappointment. Moving the cockpit rearward significantly reduced forward visibility in the landing approach to the carrier and on takeoff. The most disturbing and dangerous problem was the tendency of the port wing to stall suddenly and unexpectedly without warning. A torque stall on landing approach could be fatal. The oleo struts proved to be too stiff, leading to a pronounced bounce on landing aboard the carrier. After landing, the Corsair was directionally unstable.

Capt Eric Brown, the renowned Fleet Air Arm test pilot, judged the Corsair's landing characteristics as "really bad." An experienced pilot could cope with the early F4U's idiosyncrasies, but newly minted pilots would have their hands full landing a Corsair on a carrier. The US Navy had no choice but to disqualify the Corsair for carrier operations until these problems had been addressed. In the interim, production aircraft went to the US Marine Corps to replace the F4F-4 Wildcat for operations from land bases. "Marine Air" squadrons were delighted to receive an aircraft with superior performance to the Mitsubishi A6M Zero-sen, and the outstanding achievements of US Marine Corps fighter pilots in the fierce aerial battles over the Solomon Islands has been well documented.

The technical development of the F4U Corsair is a story of the continued and ultimately successful effort to qualify the airplane for carrier operations, improve its

After disappointing carrier-landing trials in late 1942 the US Navy declared the Corsair unsuitable for carrier operations. Lieutenant Commander "Swede" Vejtasa, an experienced pilot and F4F Wildcat ace, tested the Corsair onboard USS *Enterprise* (CV-6) and was less than pleased, coming up with a list of 18 concerns. (RG80, 80-G-62076, NARA)

capabilities and performance and increase production, all of which were achieved by the end of the war. Turning the Corsair into an acceptable carrier fighter involved numerous incremental changes, and took nearly two years. Despite its deficient landing characteristics, the Royal Navy's Fleet Air Arm accepted the Corsair for carrier duty nine months before the US Navy. Fleet Air Arm pilots developed a curving approach to landing on a carrier that kept the flightdeck in view for a longer period, facilitating better landings – US Navy and US Marine Corps pilots later adopted this technique.

A change to a bubble canopy improved visibility for landing, and for combat. An extended tail-wheel improved visibility on landing and directional stability on the ground. Further improvement in visibility came from raising the pilot's seat seven inches and increasing the vertical adjustment. Vought spent considerable effort working on modifications to the Corsair's oleo struts. The struts were re-designed with improved oil valves and increased air pressure to reduce the tendency for the fighter to bounce on landing. The solution to the stalling problem was a simple fix – a small wooden spoiler was attached to the leading edge of the starboard wing outboard of the machine guns. This affected the airflow over the starboard wing, allowing both wings to stall at the same time. With these improvements, the Corsair's landing characteristics were judged acceptable, and in April 1944 the US Navy approved the Corsair for carrier operations.

The F4U-1D model incorporated a number of improvements to enhance the capabilities of the Corsair as a fighter-bomber. Modifications in the field enabled the airplane to carry bombs under the wing center sections, allowing US Marine Corps Corsair squadrons to commence flying close air support and strike missions during the Southwest and Central Pacific campaigns. Vought developed streamlined pylons that

Given to the US Marine Corps for operation from land bases, the Corsair did sterling work in the South Pacific. Here, an F4U-1 gets prepped for takeoff from Guadalcanal in June 1943. Note the tape over the gun ports to keep barrels clean.
(Eric Hammel)

fitted under the wing center sections that could carry a 1,000lb bomb or a 150-gallon drop tank, or combinations of the two. Later, zero-length rocket launcher stubs were installed in the wings, allowing the airplane to carry four folding-fin aerial rockets (FFARs) or high velocity aircraft rockets (HVARs) under each outer wing section. These weapons considerably enhanced the Corsair's capacity for ground attack. A new cockpit canopy with a "bubble" hood and the frames removed improved visibility. The F4U-1D became the first Corsair to serve onboard US Navy carriers in significant numbers.

Pratt & Whitney, in the meantime, had continued work on the R-2800 Double Wasp engine to gain more power. A major redesign produced the R-2800-18W version, producing 2,100hp on takeoff and 2,380hp in War Emergency Power with water-menthol injection. A standard F4U-1A was converted to the prototype XF4U-4 with the newer engine, and this airplane made its first flight on April 19, 1944. With more power, the XF4U-4 achieved a top speed of 446mph – some 30mph faster than the F4U-1D. The increase in performance was so impressive that the US Navy decided to reserve production of the R-2800-18W for the F4U-4 and the new Grumman XF8F Bearcat, rather than re-engine the Grumman F6F Hellcat. The F4U-4 also featured a redesigned cockpit for greater pilot comfort and easier workload, introducing a cockpit floor. The first production version of the F4U-4 flew in September 1944.

Technical improvements would have meant little during the war without the capacity to produce aircraft in quantity, and in this area the American aviation industry proved superior to Japan. The US Navy had wisely decided before the outbreak of the Pacific War to expand production of the Corsair through license production. While its experience with the Brewster Aeronautical Corporation proved disappointing – the company suffered from chronic mismanagement that resulted in just 735 F3A-1 aircraft being produced, leading the US Navy to cancel its remaining contracts in July 1944 – the Goodyear Aircraft Corporation became a major builder of the Corsair. Vought delivered 2,814 F4U-1 and -1A aircraft, with Goodyear building an additional 2,010 similar FG-1s. Both companies then switched to the -1D model, Vought building 1,685 F4U-1Ds and Goodyear 1,997 FG-1Ds. Vought shifted to producing the F4U-4 in early 1945, building nearly 2,000 before the end of the war. In total, Vought, Brewster and Goodyear built 11,484 Corsairs before the war ended on August 15, 1945 – more than three times the number of Type 4 fighters delivered to the JAAF by Nakajima.

The XF4U-4 Corsair had the more powerful Pratt & Whitney R-2800-18W engine. Vought ceased production of the F4U-1D in February 1945 and switched to the F4U-4. Orders for 3,900 "Dash Fours" were canceled at the end of the war. (RG80, 80-G-49341, NARA)

15

F4U-1C CORSAIR

33ft 4in.

16ft 1in.

313

40ft 11in.

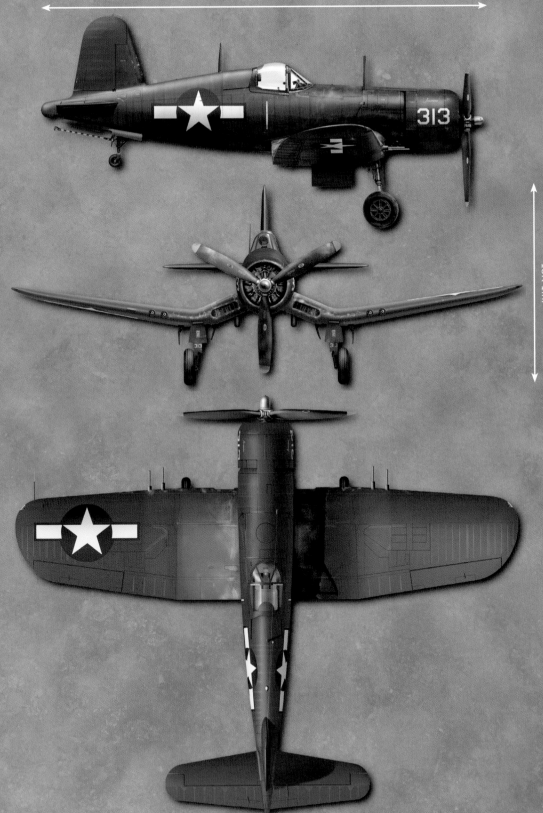

During the summer of 1945 the F4U-4 Corsair began to replace the F4U-1D/ FG-1D in US Marine Corps and US Navy fighter squadrons. The three units of MAG-14, VMF-212, VMF-222 and VMF-223, flew F4U-4s from Okinawa during the final months of the Pacific War, as did VBF-6 on board USS *Hancock* (CV-19), VBF-86 embarked in USS *Wasp* (CV-18) and VBF-94 on board USS *Lexington* (CV-16).

NAKAJIMA TYPE 4 FIGHTER Ki-84 HAYATE

The Hayate emerged from the evolution of the Rikugun Kōkū Hombu's (Army Air Headquarters) requirements for JAAF fighter airplanes and the availability of more powerful air-cooled radial engines. Over several years, based on combat experience and reports on the aerial engagements of other air forces, the Kōkū Hombu revised its thinking on the qualities required in fighter aircraft. Although lagging behind American aircraft engine development, Japanese engine manufacturers were beginning to produce airplane engines with the greater power needed to meet the demands of more advanced fighter designs by the outbreak of the Pacific War.

In 1938 the Kōkū Hombu implemented a policy of developing light and heavy single-seat fighters. The light fighter was to be exceptionally maneuverable, but lightly armed with two rifle-calibre machine guns. The light fighter reflected JAAF pilots' obsession with maneuverability – they believed the ability to maneuver in close for a kill reduced the need for heavy armament. The heavy fighter was to have multiple machine guns and cannon, with less emphasis on maneuverability and more on speed and rate of climb.

The Nakajima Hikoki K.K. (Nakajima Aircraft Company) was then developing a replacement to its successful Type 97 Fighter. The Type 1 Fighter Ki-43 Hayabusa (Falcon) was a light single-seat aircraft, with the intended armament of two 12.7mm Type 1 Ho-103 machine guns. In the summer of 1939 the company began work on a heavy fighter design as a specialized interceptor fighter. Designated the Type 2 Fighter Ki-44 Shoki (Devil-Queller), this airplane was both faster than the Ki-43 and fitted with heavier armament of two 7.7mm Type 89 Model 2 machine guns and two 12.7mm machine guns. The heavier fighter would intercept enemy bombers while the light fighter achieved air superiority over the battlefield.

After battles against the Soviet Red Air Force over the Nomonhan region during the summer of 1939, some JAAF pilots questioned the emphasis on maneuverability. The Type 97 fighters had difficulty coping with the climb and dive tactics and higher speeds of the Polikarpov I-16 and its superior armament of four 7.7mm machine guns, as well as the fast all-metal SB-2 bombers. A number of JAAF pilots returned from combat over the Nomonhan demanding fighters with higher speed and heavier armament. Other Western fighter designs were demonstrating a move toward higher speeds and heavier armament. Still, the preference for maneuverability remained, and the concept of light and heavy fighters continued to influence fighter design in the form of the Kawasaki Ki-60 and Ki-61 with inline liquid-cooled engines.

Nakajima's Ki-43 Hayabusa epitomized the "light fighter" concept – the belief in the primacy of maneuverability in the battle for air superiority. It sacrificed structural strength, armor protection and armament to equal the maneuverability of its predecessor, the Type 97 Fighter (Ki-27). These brand new Ki-43-IIs were issued to the 64th Hikō Sentai's 2nd Chutai in Palembang in August 1943. (64th Hikō Sentai Association)

Toward the end of 1941 as the Type 1 Fighter was entering service, the Kōkū Hombu began considering the need for its replacement. If the JAAF was to combat the advanced Allied fighters then under development, an airplane with considerably better performance than the Type 1 Fighter was required. The development staff within the Kōkū Hombu realized that in the confusion of combat it would be difficult to separate the mission of a pure air superiority fighter from that of a pure interceptor fighter. Inevitably, a lightly armed air superiority fighter would encounter enemy heavy bombers and an interceptor fighter would face enemy fighters. What the JAAF needed was a multi-purpose fighter combining the maneuverability of the Type 1 Fighter with the speed and heavier armament of the Type 2 Fighter.

To survive in combat with advanced Western fighter airplanes the new JAAF fighter would need self-sealing fuel tanks and greater armor protection for the pilot and systems, items the Type 1 Fighter had sacrificed in pursuit of lighter weight and greater maneuverability. Higher speed, heavier armament and better protection for fuel and the pilot meant an airplane of greater size and weight, and that would require the development of a more powerful engine.

As described in Osprey Duel 62 - *F6F Hellcat vs A6M5/7 Zero-sen*, the Japanese aviation industry lagged behind its American counterpart in the development of high-power airplane engines. Japan's two principal airplane manufacturers, the Nakajima Airplane Company and the Mitsubishi Kokuki K.K. (Mitsubishi Aircraft Company), were also the principal designers and builders of aircraft engines for the JAAF and the IJNAF.

Both companies had started out producing foreign engines under license to gain experience. Nakajima's first air-cooled radial engine was the license-built Bristol Jupiter, which it built for both civil and military uses, before developing its own air-cooled radial designs in the early 1930s. Nakajima designed and built the JAAF-designated Ha-1, a nine-cylinder engine of 780hp for the Type 97 Fighter. The company went on to create air-cooled radial engines of progressively greater power. Its first 14-cylinder engine, the famous Sakae (Prosperity), initially of 990hp, was pushed

to 1,130hp in later models. This engine powered the JAAF's Ki-43 as the Ha-115 and the IJNAF's Type 0 Fighter Zero-sen. For the Ki-44, Nakajima developed the more powerful 14-cylinder JAAF Ha-109 engine that produced 1,440hp in its first versions.

In 1940, as the Pratt & Whitney R-2800 was just commencing flight trials with the Vought XF4U Corsair, Nakajima began work on its own design for an 18-cylinder engine that would provide greater power than the Ha-109. This became the Homare (Honour), certified in 1941 and used by both the JAAF as the Ha-45 and the IJNAF as the NK9. The Homare was an exceptional design, with a small frontal section – its diameter was only 1.5 inches greater than the Sakae. The engine produced nearly 700hp more than the Sakae in its early versions for a modest increase in weight. Thus, when the Kōkū Hombu began to consider its requirements for a new JAAF fighter, there was an engine available that could provide 1,800hp, with the potential for more power with further development.

In late December 1941, the Kōkū Hombu issued its requirements for a new fighter to Nakajima. The specification called for a fighter with good maneuverability, but with greater speed and heavier armament than either the Type 1 or Type 2 Fighters. Specifically, the Kōkū Hombu wanted a top speed of 400-420mph, the ability to climb to 15,000ft in under five minutes, good range and an armament of two 12.7mm machine guns in the nose and two 20mm Type 1 Ho-5 cannon in the wings. The new fighter was to be strongly built, with armor protection for the pilot and self-sealing fuel tanks, but the Kōkū Hombu insisted it had to take fewer hours to build than the Type 1 Fighter. The powerplant was to be the new Ha-45 Homare engine.

Nakajima assigned Yasushi Koyama, who had experience with the design of the Type 97, Type 1 and Type 2 Fighters, as chief designer. By the spring of 1942 Koyama and his team had completed a design for an all-metal, low-wing monoplane with the specified armament, an enclosed cockpit providing good all-round visibility for the pilot and widely spread, retractable, landing gear and a retractable tail-wheel. In late May the Kōkū Hombu approved the design as the Ki-84.

The Nakajima Type 2 Fighter Ki-44 Shoki ("Tojo"), designed for the "heavy fighter" role to intercept enemy bombers, boasted heavier armament and emphasized speed and rate of climb over maneuverability. These Type 2 Fighters were assigned to the 47th Hikō Sentai in October 1943. (Peter M. Bowers Collection, Museum of Flight)

By November 1942 the company had built a full-scale wooden mock-up for the JAAF to evaluate. At the review meeting at the Nakajima plant in Ota, the design team asked the JAAF representatives how many test airplanes the company should plan on building. Maj Yoshitsugu Aramaki, from the Kōkū Hombu's Experimental Division responsible for the Ki-84, stunned the design team and his colleagues by recommending that Nakajima produce 100 test examples! This number was unheard of. Nakajima had built only 13 test airplanes for the Type 1 Fighter and ten for the Type 2. However, Maj Aramaki's reasoning was sound. It had taken Nakajima nearly two-and-a-half years to develop the Hayabusa and two years to develop the Shoki. Aramaki knew that by the fall of 1942 Japan did not have that amount of time. As he explained in a postwar interview:

We test pilots flew test airplanes and we'd say "this needs fixing or that needs fixing". The company worked to meet our demands, but it took many months to fix one thing. During that time the inspection process stopped there and didn't move on. That was fine in peacetime, but this was during the war. We'd already seen the limits of the Hayabusa, the Shoki and Hien [Kawasaki Type 3 Fighter Ki-61]. We needed to get the Ki-84 on the frontline of the battle as soon as possible. If we had 100 test airplanes, we could make revisions while we used it for training. If we could work on these multiple tasks at the same time, we could shorten the time it took from trial period to approval. I also thought the factory could better prepare for its mass production.

The Kōkū Hombu agreed with Maj Aramaki's recommendation, taking the unprecedented step of ordering 125 test and pre-production airplanes in two batches.

Nakajima completed the first prototype of the Ki-84 towards the end of March 1943 at its main plant at Ota, using the Ha-45 Model 11 version of the Homare engine rated at 1,900 hp. In April the new fighter made its first flight with Tsuruhisa Yoshizawa, Nakajima's test pilot, at the controls. The flight lasted 40 minutes, encountering only minor problems with the extension of the battle flaps – easily remedied that same day. Yoshizawa was more than satisfied with the results of the first test flights. After the war he recalled his first impressions of the Ki-84:

The second prototype of the Type 4 Fighter. The Hayate was intended to combine the heavier armament of the "heavy fighter" with the excellent maneuverability of the "light fighter," but with superior performance from the more powerful 1,800hp Nakajima Ho-45 Homare engine. This aircraft was photographed whilst being evaluated by the Tachikawa Air Arsenal. (Robert Lawson Collection, National Naval Aviation Museum)

It felt very similar to the Ki-43. I thought this was a bigger horsepower version of the Ki-43. Other than it was a larger airplane than the Ki-43, it didn't seem particularly different, but when I got inside the cockpit, it was very spacious from being equipped with the larger engine.

Nakajima sent the prototype to the JAAF's flight test center near Tokyo, where the Ki-84 soon demonstrated a maximum speed of 387mph – the first JAAF fighter to achieve such a figure in level flight. While the Ki-84 prototype failed to meet the JAAF's requirements for rate of climb, its general handling qualities and performance were impressive. The Ki-84 demonstrated better harmony between speed and turning ability than the Hayabusa, and it was also faster, had heavier armament and enjoyed superior performance at higher altitudes than the Shoki. However, as more prototypes entered testing, problems emerged with the Homare engine that would plague the Ki-84 throughout its life.

The engines of the first few prototypes were effectively hand-built and apparently worked well. But later prototypes with mass-produced Homare engines encountered increasing problems with excessive cylinder temperatures at full power. The cylinders functioned smoothly when operating at less than full power, but this prevented the Ki-84 from attaining peak performance. Although these issues appeared to be caused by the carburetor system, extensive testing over the summer of 1943 failed to provide a solution. There were additional problems with the oil pressure dropping at high altitude and a malfunctioning fuel system that were not resolved until later versions of the Homare engine were introduced near war's end. Testing did reveal that the engine problems went away when the Ki-84 used higher octane gasoline, as Nakajima test pilot Yoshizawa recalled:

The Ki-84 used 92 octane gasoline. When we used 100 octane gasoline that the Navy stored in Taiwan, all the engine problems stopped. It was obvious that the troubles were caused by the fuel, but it was not easy to obtain such high octane fuel then. So we kept using low octane fuel. We revised the carburretor. One hot cylinder would function normally when it was up in the air, but then other cylinders' temperatures would start to rise. It was like playing cat and mouse.

The Ki-84 also developed problems with the main landing gear, which were thought to have insufficient strength, although Yoshizawa believed that any perceived weakness in the undercarriage was due more to pilot ability:

Later, in the battle area, the Ki-84 gained a reputation for having fragile landing gear that broke easily. Unfortunately, this was mostly related to the pilots' lack of flying skills. It is understandable that they were flustered by an airplane with such large horsepower, after only having a short amount of time being taught in training airplanes such as the Type 95 [Tachikawa Type 95 Ki-9 Medium Grade Trainer]. The situation made it difficult to fly calmly, and as you got frustrated you made basic mistakes. On top of that, it was hard for the Ki-84's tail-wheel to make contact with the ground even after you landed, so it always landed with a thump. This was hard to handle, so pilots just got frustrated and ended up breaking the landing gear. But problems like these we could

manage. We truly suffered from the engine issues, however. The Ki-84's weak point was the engine, which we had the most difficult time with, and it never worked properly right until the end. It was really disappointing that we could only operate it by tricking the engine to work, and to gain speed that way.

With the JAAF anxious to get the new fighter into production as quickly as possible, these problems were overlooked and, in April 1944 – just a year after its first flight – the Ki-84 was accepted for service by the Kōkū Hombu as the Type 4 Fighter Model A (Ki-84 Ko, or Ki-84a). Ordered to commence full-scale production, Nakajima had by then built 83 Ki-84s in the first pre-production batch. In addition to supplementing the test program, a number of these aircraft went to a special operational test unit formed at the end of 1943. Another 42 aircraft in the second pre-production batch had been completed by June 1944.

Three months earlier, the 22nd Hikō Sentai had become the first JAAF air regiment to re-equip with the Type 4 Fighter, taking its airplanes to China in August for the Ki-84's successful combat debut against the USAAF's Fourteenth Air Force. In April three more fighter Sentai were established with the Ki-84, followed by a further three in May and three more in August. Older established Sentai like the 25th and 85th Hikō Sentai in China and the 50th Hikō Sentai in Burma also converted to the Ki-84 during the summer and fall. The Type 4 fighter found its way to the Rensei Hikotai

(Operational Training Units) and other JAAF flying schools too. At last the Japanese had a fighter that could, in experienced hands, match the performance of its Allied counterparts. However, while the Ki-84 showed a definite qualitative improvement over other JAAF fighters, at this stage of the war it was quantity and pilot skill that mattered almost as much, and here the JAAF fell short.

It was unfortunate for the JAAF that production of the Type 4 Fighter began just as Japan's wartime industrial production was peaking, and about to enter an irreversible decline. The Japanese aviation industry's increase in production from 1942 until the middle of 1944 was an impressive achievement. Aircraft production grew nearly three-fold and aircraft engine production nearly doubled in two years, with a tripling of the work force, but production peaked in June 1944 and declined thereafter. The Japanese aviation industry had not fully mastered the techniques of mass production, so that in many factories handwork methods predominated. As the war went on, shortages of skilled workers hampered production. Increasing American air attacks on Nakajima's factories in the fall of 1944 forced the company to begin dispersing its production away from its main plants, further disrupting the delivery of aircraft.

The majority of Type 4 fighters were built at Nakajima's Ota plant in Gunma prefecture, northeast of Tokyo. In May 1944 a second production line opened at Nakajima's factory at Utsonomiya, in Tochigi prefecture. Production of the Ki-84 peaked in December 1944, and although the 1,904 aircraft built by Nakajima during 1944 were less than the Kōkū Hombu had planned, it was still a remarkable achievement. In total, Nakajima completed approximately 3,416 Ki-84 aircraft from November 1943 through to war's end, compared to 5,919 Type 1 Fighters built from 1941 to 1945. Production at Ota suffered when the plant was severely damaged in an air raid on February 10, 1945. A third source of production was the Manshu Hikoki Seizo K.K. plant in Manchuria, which began building the Ki-84 in 1945 – it had completed just 95 aircraft by VJ Day.

What affected production of the Ki-84 most of all in the final months of the Pacific War was the decline in engine production and engine quality. The catastrophic

Ki-84s captured in the Philippines gave the Allied Technical Air Intelligence Unit its first opportunity to examine the JAAF's new fighter and to draw accurate recognition diagrams for Allied pilots. (RG80, 80-G-194752f, NARA)

OPPOSITE

This three-view shows a Ki-84-I Hayate from the 103rd Hikō Sentai. This unit was formed in central Honshu during August 1944, and together with the 101st and 102nd Hikō Sentai it made up the 100th Hikōdan (Air Brigade). The 103rd began training with the Type 1 Fighter (Ki-43 "Oscar") prior to receiving its first Hayates in October. The unit initially served on home defense duties, countering the B-29 raids from Okinawa. In March 1945 the 100th Hikōdan's three Sentai moved to bases on Kyushu in preparation for the expected attack on the Ryukyus, coming under the command of the 6th Kōkūgun. After the invasion of Okinawa the 103rd Hikō Sentai flew patrols in defense of airfields on Kyushu and escorted the Shimbu-Tai Special Attack units. On an escort mission on May 4, 1945, Maj Michiaki Tojo, Sentai commander, claimed two F4U Corsairs shot down.

A formation of Ki-84s from the 101st Sentai prepares to take off on a mission from their base at Miyakonojo, on the island, of Kyushu in 1945. The 101st was heavily involved in escorting JAAF Shimbu-tai (Special Attack) units on their missions to Okinawa. (Dr. Yasuho Izawa)

shipping losses cut Japan off from sources of the critical metals used in engine manufacture, such as molybdenum and nickel. Engine production fell sharply during 1945. In the month of June 1945, Nakajima produced 168 Ki-84 aircraft but only 150 Ha-45 Homare engines.

In the production models of the Ki-84 Ko, the Ha-45 Model 12 replaced the earlier Ha-45 Model 11 engine, providing a small increase in power to 1,825hp. Late production aircraft had the more powerful Ha-45 Model 21, which was rated at 1,990hp for takeoff, or the Ha-45 Model 23 of slightly less power (1,900hp) that finally solved some of the problems associated with the fuel system. The next version of the Ki-84, the Type 4 Fighter Model B (Ki-84 Otsu, Ki-84b) featured heavier armament, with the Ho-5 20mm cannon replacing the fuselage-mounted Ho-103 12.7mm machine guns. The Type 4 Fighter Model C (Ki-84 Hei, Ki-84c) had even heavier armament, with the Ho-5 20mm cannon in the wings exchanged for the 30mm Ho-155-II cannon. Nakajima built a few prototypes of the Type 4 Fighter, possibly as the Model D, with four Ho-5 20mm cannon in the wings and fuselage and a fifth Ho-5 mounted obliquely behind the cockpit to fire at bombers from below. The last production airplanes featured the Ha-45 Model 25, this version of the Homare engine finally reaching the elusive rating of 2,000hp.

Serviceability and maintenance remained a problem throughout the Ki-84's operational life. The Homare would function well with regular and careful maintenance, but problems with the engine became even more pronounced in the field, where operating conditions, shortages of skilled groundcrew and a lack of spare parts made regular maintenance problematic. As confidence in engine quality and maintenance declined, worries about the powerplant increased. Difficulties with the hydraulic system and the landing gear, especially when less-experienced pilots flew the Ki-84, resulted in many operational accidents.

The Kōkū Hombu had hoped that the Nakajima Type 4 Fighter would redress the balance in performance with the second generation of American fighter aeroplanes. While the Hayate went a long way toward achieving this ambitious goal, the American aviation industry made another leap in engine power with the Pratt & Whitney R-2800-18W, providing the F4U Corsair with an even greater margin of performance over its Japanese rival.

Ki-84-I HAYATE

32ft 10in.

11ft 1.25in.

36ft 10in.

TECHNICAL SPECIFICATIONS

F4U CORSAIR

F4U-1D/FG-1D

The F4U Corsair was a large and heavy airplane designed and built to withstand the stresses of operating from aircraft carriers. The fuselage was constructed from aluminium panels, with internal ribs and stiffeners for added strength, that conformed as closely as possible to the diameter of the Pratt & Whitney R-2800 engine. The main 217-gallon self-sealing fuel tank was placed between the engine and the cockpit. The Corsair's distinguishing inverted gull wings were built of aluminium panels and spars, but the outer wing panels were fabric-covered and the ailerons were built from fabric-covered plywood. The rudder and horizontal stabilizers were also fabric-covered.

The Corsair had eight main sections, namely the engine, three fuselage assemblies (forward, center section and rear), inner and outer wing assemblies, landing gear and the tail assembly. The outer wing sections contained the armament and internal fuel tanks in the early F4U-1A, and they could be raised hydraulically to minimize the aircraft's footprint on the carrier deck.

The F4U-1D and the similar Goodyear-built FG-1D featured numerous improvements over the F4U-1A. The -1D model incorporated the many changes necessary to make the Corsair a suitable carrier aircraft. The starboard wing had the small wooden spoiler on the leading edge that improved the Corsair's stall characteristics, while changes to the oil valves and air pressure in the shock absorbers reduced the aircraft's tendency to bounce on landing. A lengthened tail-wheel and a reduction in the maximum deflection angle of the tail hook were additional refinements to improve the Corsair's landings on carrier decks. The -1D also incorporated the adjustable pilot's seat for better visibility. Late production models had a "bubble" canopy with the overhead frames of the F4U-1A removed. All the F4U-1D/FG-1D models had the R-2800-8W engine with water injection that provided 2,250hp at sea level in the War Emergency Power setting. About midway through the production run a new, slightly smaller diameter, Hamilton Standard propeller was introduced.

The F4U-1D/FG-1D had several features designed to enhance the Corsair's ability as a fighter-bomber, the most obvious of which were two streamlined pylons mounted on the underside of the inner wing between the fuselage and the landing gear. Each pylon could carry a 1,000lb bomb or a 150-gallon fuel tank. The -1D retained the centerline mounting for a bomb or drop tank as well, allowing for combinations of drop tanks and bombs to be carried. The provision for additional drop tanks allowed the wing fuel tanks to be removed. Later production models added four zero-length rocket launchers under each outer wing section to carry four 5in. FFARs or HVARs.

F4U-1D CORSAIR MACHINE GUNS

Like its Grumman F6F stablemate, the Corsair was armed with a battery of excellent, reliable Browning M-2 0.50in. machine guns. Three weapons were placed in each outer wing panel, with the ammunition containers located outboard of the guns. Access to the guns and ammunition containers was through panels on the upper wing. The inboard and middle guns were provided with 400 rounds of ammunition, while the outboard gun had 375 rounds. The guns were charged hydraulically with controls located in the cockpit. The high muzzle velocity of the 0.50in. round gave it good range and accuracy and the use of a single caliber of weapon with a single trajectory made sighting easier for the pilot.

F4U-1C

Although the US Navy adopted a battery of six 0.50in. machine guns as standard armament for its fighter aircraft, the Bureau of Aeronautics retained an interest in more powerful 20mm cannon and requested that Vought develop a suitably armed version of the Corsair. In August 1943 the XF4U-1C made its first flight armed with two AN-M2 20mm cannon (a license-built development of the Hispano-Suiza HS.404 autocannon) in each wing, with 231 rounds per gun. The -1C wing could also be fitted with four zero-length rocket launders to carry four rockets, but they were

Later production models of the F4U-1D/FG-1D featured four zero-length rocket launchers under each wing for FFAR or HVAR rockets. Here, a pilot from VBF-84 walks to his airplane prior to flying a mission over Kyushu in March 1945. (RG80, 80-G-312605, NARA)

The majority of Corsairs were armed with six Browning M-2 machine guns. Three weapons were housed in each outer wing panel, with the ammunition containers located outboard of the guns. Access to the guns and ammunition containers was through access panels on the upper wing. The inboard and middle guns were provided with 400 rounds of ammunition, while the outboard gun had 375 rounds. Here, an armorer from VMF-511 tends to the guns of an F4U-1D on the flightdeck of the escort carrier USS *Block Island* (CVE-21). (Tailhook Association)

not always present as standard equipment. In all other respects, the -1C was similar to the -1D model.

The -1C served with three US Marine Corps squadrons (VMF-311, VMF-314 and VMF-441) on Okinawa in 1945 and with US Navy squadrons VF-84, VBF-84, VF-85 and VBF-85 onboard the carriers USS *Bunker Hill* (CV-17) and USS *Shangri-la* (CV-38) during the final year of the war. These units experienced operating problems with the AN-M2 20mm cannon, which was plagued by misfires. Many pilots also preferred the 0.50in. machine gun for aerial combat because of its more rapid rate of fire and greater quantity of ammunition.

The F4U-1C featured two AN-M2 20mm cannon in each wing, with 231 rounds per gun. While some pilots appreciated the explosive power of the larger-caliber weapon, others preferred the greater ammunition load and increased rate of fire of the standard 0.50in. machine gun armament. (Robert Lawson Collection, National Museum of Naval Aviation)

F4U-4

The F4U-4 featured a significant improvement in performance over earlier models thanks to its more powerful Pratt & Whitney R-2800-18W engine. In an attempt to get even more power, reliability and durability out of the R-2800 engine, Pratt & Whitney engineers undertook a major redesign of the engine that became the C-series. It featured forged cylinders in place of cast cylinders, which were reaching the limits of their performance at 2,000hp, with greater cooling fin area. A new strengthened crankcase center section and a redesigned crankshaft were fitted, designed to accommodate the increase in horsepower. The R-2800-18W had a two-stage, two-speed supercharger and water-menthol injection. The -18W engine gave 2,100hp on takeoff and 2,380hp at War Emergency Power.

The demands of the new engine required a larger air scoop for the supercharger at the bottom of the cowling. The cowl flaps were redesigned and reduced in number to five on each side of the cowling in place of the 15 cowl flaps on earlier models. With the R-2800-18W and a four-bladed Hamilton Standard propeller, the F4U-4 Corsair had a maximum speed of 446mph at 26,200ft – some 30mph faster than the earlier F4U-1D. The more powerful engine improved the Corsair's rate of climb as well, with the F4U-4 capable of reaching 20,000ft in 5.9 minutes (without bombs or drop tanks) compared to 7.7 minutes in the F4U-1D.

Vought took the opportunity to make changes in the cockpit for added pilot comfort and to increase the Corsair's armor protection. To the delight of pilots, Vought replaced the foot rails of the earlier models, which allowed dirt and whatever else might have been dropped in the fuselage to join the pilot whenever the airplane was inverted, with a cockpit floor. The pilot's seat was redesigned, and featured armrests, the control column was shortened and the rudder pedals revised. For greater protection, a bulletproof laminated glass plate was placed under the front windshield and an armor plate fitted in front of the instrument panel, with armor plates behind the pilot's seat widened to the width of the fuselage. Additional armor plating was placed underneath the engine.

The -4 model retained the two underwing pylons for drop tanks or bombs, but removed the centerline attachment points. The four zero-length rocket launchers under each outer wing were retained. Armament remained the standard six 0.50in. Browning M-2 machine guns with 2,400 rounds.

Ki-84 HAYATE

TYPE 4 FIGHTER MODEL A (Ki-84 Ko) HAYATE

The first model of the Type 4 Fighter to enter service, the Model A (Ki-84 Ko) was larger and heavier than the Type I Fighter (Ki-43) it replaced – its maximum takeoff weight was some 2,700lbs greater than the Hayabusa. A stronger and more robust aircraft than the Type 1, the Hayate had a higher diving speed and could execute more demanding maneuvers than the earlier fighter.

The relatively small diameter of the Ha-45 Homare engine enabled Yasushi Koyama and his team to design a superbly streamlined oval-shaped fuselage, with the engine

enclosed in a tight-fitting cowling. The fuselage and wing were all-metal, with a light alloy stressed-skin covering. The fuselage held a 35-gallon water-menthol tank ahead of the cockpit, with a fuel tank mounted behind. This main tank and two tanks in each wing held 162 gallons of fuel. The cockpit sat above and just behind the low wing. An adjustable seat allowed good visibility for takeoff out of the three-piece canopy. A 65mm armored glass block behind the windscreen in front and 13mm armor plate behind the pilot's seat provided protection for the pilot.

With its two fuselage-mounted Ho-113 12.7mm machine guns firing through the propeller and two wing-mounted Ho-5 20mm cannon (considered one of the best 20mm aircraft cannon fielded by either side during the war), the Type 4 Fighter had a much heavier weight of fire than the Type 1 Fighter – vitally necessary for engaging strongly built American fighters. The belt-fed Ho-113 machine guns had a rate of fire of 800–900 rounds per minute, with 350 rounds for each gun. The Ho-5 cannon had a slightly lower rate of fire of 750–850 rounds per minute. The wings of the Type 4 held 150 belt-fed rounds for each Ho-5 cannon.

In common with many other Japanese fighters, Nakajima built the wing of the Type 4 integral with the central fuselage. A strongly built heavy main spar contributed to the airplane's strength. An auxiliary spar supported the metal-skinned wings, which had fabric-covered ailerons. The flaps could be lowered 15 degrees to improve maneuverability in combat. Racks under the wings could carry 44-gallon drop tanks or 250kg bombs. The wings held two more fuel tanks, with self-sealing protection, inboard of the landing gear and two smaller tanks in the wing leading edge.

Ki-84 HAYATE COWLING/WING GUNS

The Type 4 Fighter was equipped with two 12.7mm Ho-103 machine guns in the nose, synchronized to fire through the propeller. Ammunition for the nose guns consisted of belts of 350 rounds stored in ammunition containers beneath the guns in the fuselage. Based on the Browning machine gun, the Ho-103 had a higher rate of fire than its American counterpart, but fired a lighter-weight cartridge. The wings held two Ho-5 20mm cannon, which had a superior rate of fire to the IJNAF's Type 99-2. Like the Ho-103, the Ho-5 was belt-fed, with containers in the wings for the ammunition holding 150 rounds. These containers were accessible through panels in the upper wing surface.

The first production models of the Type 4 Fighter used the Ha-45 Model 11 engine, providing 1,800hp for takeoff. Later versions changed to the Ha-45 Model 12, Model 21 and Model 23, which gave slightly greater horsepower in each model. Although the prototype Ki-84 could reach 5,000m (16,405ft) in 5 min 54 sec, this still did not meet the Kōkū Hombu's demanding specification. With full armament and armor protection, the time to 5,000m slipped to 6 min 26 sec, leading some pilots to state that the Type 4 lacked sufficient power on account of the Homare engine producing less than 2,000hp. As with so many other fighters, extra equipment in the form of weaponry, armored protection and fuel, with little additional horsepower to offset them, reduced performance. The difficulty of getting the Homare engine to operate reliably at full power only compounded the problem.

During 1944 the JAAF established several new fighter Sentai to be equipped with the Ki-84, as well as re-equipping several existing units. The 73rd Hikō Sentai, shown here, was formed in May 1944 and fought in the home defence role after seeing combat in the Philippines campaign. (Peter M. Bowers Collection, Museum of Flight)

TYPE 4 FIGHTER MODEL B (OTSU)

The main differences between the Type 4 Model A (Ki-84 Ko or Ki-84a) and the Type 4 Model B (Ki-84 Otsu or Ki-84b) centered on armament and engine fitment. The Model B featured four Ho-5 20mm cannon, with two cannon replacing the Ho-113 12.7mm machine guns mounted in the fuselage. This was intended to give the Type 4 more powerful armament for attacking USAAF B-29 bombers over Japan. The Model B was built in fewer numbers than the Type 4 Fighter Model A, production probably amounting to only several hundred aircraft. The last aircraft to be built were fitted with the final version of the Homare engine, the Ha-45 Model 25 rated at 2,000hp.

F4U-1D and Ki-84 Comparison Specifications		
	F4U-1D	**Ki-84**
Powerplant	2,000 hp Pratt & Whitney R-2800	1,900hp Nakajima *Homare* Ha-45-21
Dimensions		
Span	40ft 11in.	36ft 10^7/16in.
Length	33ft 4in.	32ft 6^9/16in.
Height	16ft 1in.	11ft 1^1/4in.
Wing Area	314sq. ft	226sq. ft
Weights		
Empty	8,982lb	5,864lb
Loaded	11,962lb	7,955lb
Performance		
Max Speed	417mph at 19,000ft	392mph at 20,080ft
Range	1,015 miles	1,053 miles
Climb Rate at Sea Level	2,890ft/min at military power	3,790ft/min at military power
Service Ceiling	36,900ft	34,450ft
Armament	6 x 0.50in. Browning M-2 machine guns	2 x Ho-103 12.7mm machine guns 2 x Ho-5 20mm cannon

THE STRATEGIC SITUATION

In January 1945, Japan's strategic military and economic situation was dire. With the invasion of Luzon on January 9, American forces had effectively gained control over the Philippines, and could now threaten Japan's sea links to the vital raw materials of Southeast Asia. US Navy submarines had already inflicted crippling losses on Japanese merchant shipping, leaving the country dependent on its remaining stocks of fuel and metals. Imports of oil stopped in December 1944, and by the spring of 1945 aircraft production had dropped by one-third and aircraft engine production by two-thirds. The Japanese economy was failing.

The defense of the Philippines had cost the JAAF and IJNAF thousands of airplanes and pilots, the bulk of the Imperial Japanese Navy's remaining capital ships and tens of thousands of troops. Japan's Imperial General Headquarters realized that the next stage of the American advance would be an attack on the nation's inner defensive ring – most likely an attempt to capture Okinawa, in the Ryukyu Islands, to use as a base for the invasion of Japan. Imperial General Headquarters decided to prepare Japan for what were likely to be intensive air attacks from USAAF B-29s in the Marianas as a prelude to invasion. Japan's only hope of survival was to inflict such punishing losses on Allied forces that they would be forced to withdraw. Formosa, the Bonin Islands and Okinawa were to be held to the last man.

For the defense of Okinawa, designated Operation *"Ten-Go"*, Imperial General Headquarters re-organized Japan's air defenses. Responsibility for countering American air raids on the main island of Honshu fell to the Tokyo-based 1st Kōkūgun (1st Air Army) with the 10th, 11th and 12th Hikō Shidan (Air Divisions) and the IJNAF's

Home Defense Force, with some 500 aircraft in total. To protect the approaches to the Home Islands, the 6th Kōkūgun and 3rd, 5th and 10th Kōkū Kantai (Air Fleet) in Japan and the 8th Kōkūgun and 1st Kōkū Kantai in Formosa had approximately 4,600 aircraft.

Because of insufficient numbers of advanced fighter airplanes like the Type 4 Fighter Hayate and the IJNAF's Navy's N1K2-J Shiden-Kai, the lack of experienced pilots following losses in the Philippines and the impossibility of completing training of the new intake of pilot trainees before the likely date of an American attack, the JAAF and IJNAF decided to rely on mass kamikaze

attacks to destroy the invasion fleet. Both services converted entire training classes into Tokubetsu Kōgeki Tai (Special Attack Units), the 10th Kōkū Kantai becoming almost exclusively a Special Attack force.

American military planners believed that the only way to force Japan to accept unconditional surrender was through the invasion of the Home Islands. With the seizure of the Philippines to provide a base for the fleet, the need to invade Formosa diminished. To save time and resources, the American Joint Chiefs of Staff decided instead to move forward with the capture of Iwo Jima, in the Bonin Islands, as an advanced base for fighters to escort the B-29s over Japan, and then to take Okinawa as a base for the planned invasion of Kyushu, scheduled for November 1945. Fighters and medium bombers could reach Kyushu from Okinawa to soften up Japanese defenses prior to the invasion.

Designated Operation *Iceberg*, the invasion of Okinawa would involve a massive force of 541,000 men in four US Army and three US Marine Corps divisions. They would be supported by the US Navy's Fifth Fleet, with an invasion covering force and Task Force (TF) 58 – the Fast Carrier Task Force – providing air cover until land-based US Marine Corps and USAAF units could take over using captured Okinawan airfields. For the initial invasion, TF 58 had 11 Essex-class fleet carriers and six Independence-class light carriers. Waiting in the wings were the squadrons of the 2nd Marine Aircraft Wing (MAW).

To counter the kamikaze threat, the US Navy increased the number of fighters aboard the Essex-class fleet carriers from 54 to 73, cutting back bomber and torpedo airplanes to 15 apiece. These enlarged fighter squadrons proved too difficult to administer, so on January 2, 1945 the US Navy divided these squadrons into two – a fighter squadron (VF) and a fighter-bomber squadron (VBF). This gave the carrier groups more airplanes for CAPs to protect the fleet, while the fighter-bombers made up for the cuts in the number of bomber airplanes. More critically, the US Navy needed fighters that were faster and had a better rate of climb than the F6F-5 Hellcat. Fortunately, the Corsair, some 30mph faster than the Hellcat, was available. The US Navy had begun converting several fighter squadrons to the Corsair in the fall of 1944, but to speed up re-equipping the fleet carriers the US Marine Corps was asked to provide Corsair squadrons for service aboard the vessels, VMF-124 and VMF-213

The JAAF and IJNAF suffered heavy losses while attempting to defend the Philippines from American invasion. The loss of so many experienced pilots led to the decision to mount mass kamikaze attacks in the battle for Okinawa. Here, a Nakajima B6N2 Navy Carrier Attack Bomber Tenzan (code-named "Jill") or C6N1 Navy Carrier Reconnaissance Plane Saiun (code-named "Myrt") falls under the guns of an F6F Hellcat. This airplane was claimed as a "Zeke," illustrating the difficulties of aircraft recognition in the heat of combat. (RG80, 80-G-46983, NARA)

TBM Avengers and SB2C Helldivers of Carrier Air Group 17 on their way to Okinawa in April 1945. The aircraft carriers of TF 58 covered the Okinawa invasion force, targeting airfields on Kyushu, providing support to US Army and US Marines Corps forces on the ground and flying CAPs against the kamikaze. (RG80, 80-G-314365, NARA)

embarking in USS *Essex* (CV-9) in January 1945. For the Okinawa campaign, TF 58 had five US Navy and six US Marine Corps Corsair squadrons.

The battle for Okinawa lasted 11 weeks. Operation *"Ten-Go"* proved to be a failure, the JAAF and IJNAF launching ten Kikusui (Floating Chrysanthemum) attacks that saw 1,465 Special Attack aircraft and their crews lost. In total, the JAAF and IJNAF had approximately 3,000 airplanes destroyed attempting to defeat the American invasion of Okinawa. The JAAF used its more experienced pilots and better aircraft on sweeps to clear a path for the Special Attack units making their way to Okinawa, where the Tokubetsu Tai sought out transport vessels, while their IJNAF counterparts went after the US Navy's fleet units. The carrier air groups of TF 58 (and, belatedly, B-29s from the Marianas) flew repeated strikes against the Special Attack bases on Kyushu and CAPs in defense of the fleet. Land-based US Marine Corps Corsair squadrons flying from Okinawa joined them as soon as airfields were secured.

With the loss of Okinawa, Japan now faced invasion. The American strategy was to undertake an air and sea blockade of Japan, cutting the nation off from all imports of fuel, raw materials and food to weaken its capacity to make war. The B-29s of the Twentieth Air Force would continue their campaign against industrial cities, aircraft factories and oil refineries, adding mining the waters of the Inland Sea to their missions. A steady build-up of US Marine Corps and USAAF tactical units on Okinawa would undertake missions against targets in Kyushu. The US Navy's Fast Carrier Task Force (supported by the British Pacific Fleet), initially under the command of Admiral William Halsey as TF 38 (as TF 58 was designated when under his leadership), would undertake strikes along the Japanese coast, attacking airfields, shipping, industrial plants and wearing down JAAF and IJNAF air strength through attrition. Operation *Olympic* – the invasion of Kyushu – was planned for November 1, 1945, involving more than 50 US Army and US Marine Corps divisions and aircraft

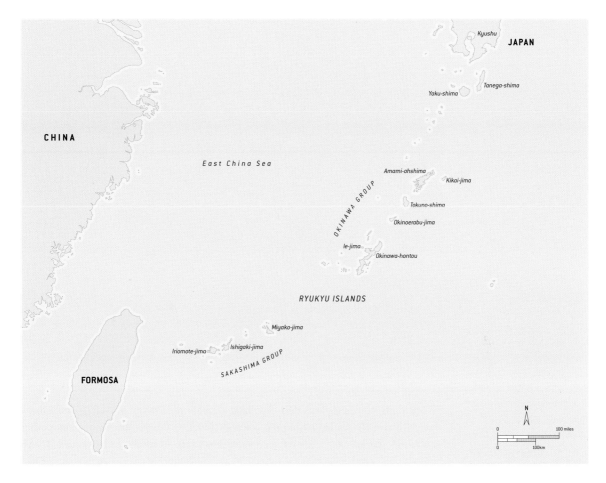

The battleground for the Okinawa campaign stretched from Kyushu, in the Home Islands, to Formosa, off the China coast. The Shimbu-Tai units were based in Kyushu and on Formosa. Their targets were the American transports anchored off the west coast of Okinawa and the carriers of TF 58 steaming to the east of the island. The Special Attack units and their escorts followed the Ryukyu Islands chain to their targets.

from the Far East Air Force (Fifth, Seventh and Thirteenth Air Forces), a Commonwealth air component and MAWs.

In the face of such overwhelming force, Imperial General Headquarters had few options for Operation *"Ketsu-Go"* – the defense of Japan. A joint JAAF-IJNAF air agreement signed on July 13, 1945 outlined the principal objectives of the air plan. The most important mission was to destroy the American invasion force while it was still on the water in the first stages of landing. For this the JAAF had amassed around 1,600 Special Attack aircraft in the 1st and 6th Kōkgun, with the expectation of preparing an additional 1,000 Special Attack aircraft from obsolete airplanes by the end of August. The IJNAF's 3rd, 5th and 10th Kōkū Kantai could muster nearly 4,000 Special Attack aircraft.

The secondary missions for both the JAAF and the IJNAF were to provide for the air defense of Japan and to disrupt American pre-invasion operations with their regular air units. For this role the 1st and 6th Kōkūgun had some 900 aircraft nominally available, including eight fighter sentai equipped with the Type 4 Fighter and five sentai re-equipping with the new Type 5 Fighter (Kawasaki Ki-100), while the IJNAF's air fleets had approximately 1,200 aircraft available.

As the air attacks on Okinawa petered out in June, Gen Masakuzu Kawabe, commander of the Japanese Army's Kōkū Shōgun (General Air Army), formed in

Only the engines remain of more than 20 Corsairs from VF-84, VMF-221 and VMF-451 following a kamikaze attack by two bomb-laden Zero-sens on USS *Bunker Hill* (CV-17) on May 11, 1945 that killed 393 men and knocked the vessel out of the war. In the expectation of more attacks during the Okinawa campaign, the US Navy increased the number of fighters aboard its fleet carriers to 72, leading to additional US Marine Corps Corsair squadrons joining the fleet. (RG80, 80-G-259964, NARA)

The intent in capturing Okinawa was to provide a base for tactical air support for the invasion of the home islands, set to begin in November 1945 with the invasion of Kyushu. By July 1945 the US Marines Corps had four MAGs on Okinawa with twelve squadrons of Corsairs. Here, "Marine Air" Corsairs taxi out at Kadena prior to flying a mission. (208-AA-PAC-Box 87-Folder K, NARA)

April to better coordinate the operations of the 1st and 6th Kōkūgun, ordered his forces to refrain from combat with intruding American fighter and bomber formations in order to rebuild the JAAF's air strength following the devastating losses over Okinawa. But USAAF air raids on Japanese aircraft factories had such a serious impact on production that Imperial General Headquarters instructed Kawabe to stop trying to conserve his aircraft and instead respond aggressively to American attacks with the forces he had available.

THE COMBATANTS

US NAVY AND US MARINE CORPS PILOT TRAINING

For a young American university graduate hoping to be a US Navy or US Marine Corps fighter pilot during 1944, the experience of training was qualitatively different than that which his Japanese counterpart received. By this stage of the war the US Navy's training system was operating efficiently and providing a comprehensive program covering flying skills, combat tactics and gunnery. In contrast to the JAAF, the US Navy's training program benefited from an adequate number of experienced instructors, unlimited fuel for flying and a steady supply of training airplanes and first-line operational aircraft. With production at high levels, there were now enough first-line fighters to provide both combat units and operational training units. The number of aircraft in the US Navy's training command peaked in 1944 at 9,652.

At the end of 1943, Naval Air Training Command was established to control all phases of training at the three subordinate commands – Primary, Intermediate and Operational Training Command. During 1944, this system trained 21,067 naval aviators for the US Navy and the US Marine Corps.

An aviation cadet began his training with three months at Flight Preparatory School, where he took classes in the basic elements of flight, navigation, maths, physics and aircraft and ship recognition. He also undertook intensive physical training. From there the aviation cadet went to a War Training Service school for three months of elementary flying training with civilian flight instructors on light airplanes such as the Piper J-3 Cub, accumulating around 40 hours of dual and solo flight time. If successful, the aviation cadet then moved to a primary training school

US Navy and US Marine Corps pilots completed their primary training on Naval Aircraft Factory N3N or Boeing N2S Stearman biplane trainers – more than two dozen examples of the latter airplane can be seen in this view. Airfields in the American south and along the Gulf Coast provided good weather for training most of the year. (Naval Air Training Command Public Affairs Office)

for up to 14 weeks of flight instruction in the Naval Aircraft Factory N3N or Boeing N2S Stearman primary training biplane. The emphasis in primary training was learning to fly the aircraft with precision, individually and as part of a formation. During primary training the aviation cadet would accumulate another 90 to 100 hours of flying time.

During the intermediate training phase the aviation cadet learned to fly heavier and more powerful airplanes in anticipation of moving on to operational aircraft. At Pensacola, in Florida, or Corpus Christi, in Texas, cadets would spend 14 to 18 weeks gaining another 160 hours of flying time. During the first part of intermediate training the cadet would fly the Vultee SNV Valiant, moving on to the North American SNJ Texan in the advanced stage. Here, a cadet selected for training as a fighter pilot would begin working on more advanced formation flying, elementary combat tactics and aerial gunnery. On completion of intermediate training the cadet would be given his wings and a commission as an ensign in the US Navy or a second lieutenant in the US Marine Corps. By this time a cadet would have acquired around 300 hours of flying time before moving to an operational training unit to become a fully qualified service pilot.

US Navy and US Marine Corps pilots destined for fighter squadrons went to one of several operational training units at fields on the southeast coast of the USA. Here, they were introduced to service airplanes, learning to fly the F4F and FM-2 Wildcat, the F6F Hellcat and the F4U Corsair. Operational training was an intensive

course in fighter tactics and gunnery, combining ground school classes and flying practice that added a further 100 flying hours to a trainee fighter pilot's logbook.

The goals of operational training were to ensure that the neophyte fighter pilot learned to fly a high-performance airplane with confidence, and practiced basic fighter maneuvers until they became second nature. The trainee learned to fly as part of a division of four airplanes – the US Navy's basic fighting formation – being taught how to fly as a wingman in support of his element leader. There was intensive practice in aerial gunnery and gunnery approaches, learning the mechanics of deflection shooting until this too became automatic. US Navy pilots would practice carrier landings and complete eight recoveries either on an escort carrier or one of the two converted passenger liners used for carrier landing practice in Lake Michigan off Chicago. By the time he completed his operational training, a US Navy or US Marine Corps pilot would have accumulated 400 to 500 hours of flying time – nearly double what his Japanese counterpart would have accrued during the same period.

Young naval aviators accumulated more flying hours and went through additional intensive combat training once they joined a squadron. By this stage of the war the US Navy and US Marine Corps had enough combat squadrons in their carrier air groups and MAGs to be able to rotate units out of the frontline for periods of rest and rebuilding. Pilots fresh from operational training would join their squadrons,

The North American SNJ Texan fulfilled the advanced training role. Trainee fighter pilots would move on to the SNJ in the second phase of their intermediate training, practicing formation flying, aerial gunnery and basic fighter tactics in the machine. (Museum of Flight)

By 1944 there were more than enough Corsairs to equip frontline squadrons and Stateside training units. These F4Us were stationed at MCAS El Toro, California, which was home to a Fighter Training Unit and facilities for squadrons training to return to combat. (Peter M. Bowers Collection, Museum of Flight)

where they would undergo more training in combat flying under the experienced eyes of veterans who had served one or more combat tours and were preparing their squadrons for their next deployment.

New pilots would be assigned to a division, where they would fly as wingmen to more experienced pilots who would train them in aerial combat, bombing, strafing and the other skills they would need when engaging the enemy. There would often be opportunities for practice dogfights with other US Navy or US Marine Corps squadrons or cooperative USAAF squadrons flying different types of fighters – invaluable experience for the beginner. In contrast to a newly trained JAAF pilot, a US Navy or US Marine Corps fighter pilot going off to combat in early 1945 would have had not just more flying hours, but better and more comprehensive practice in controlling his airplane, in air combat tactics and in aerial gunnery.

JAAF PILOT TRAINING

During the course of the Pacific War, JAAF pilot training underwent significant changes in both organizational structure and duration as a result of attrition and growing shortages of aircraft and fuel. As the war went on, shortened flying training courses and inadequate flying practice led to a steady deterioration in pilot quality. When the JAAF was finally able to introduce a superior airplane in the Type 4 Fighter, its training system was not able to produce pilots with the skills needed to take advantage of its flying and fighting qualities.

JAAF pilot trainees learned to fly on the Tachikawa Type 95-1 Medium Grade Trainer (Ki-9 "Spruce"), which served as the primary trainer throughout the Pacific War. (Author's collection)

As with most air forces, the JAAF's training scheme was divided into segments providing for progressive advancement in flying skill. After a period of ground instruction, pilot trainees would begin flight training at an elementary flying training school (hikō gakkō), where they would be taught basic flying skills in the Type 95 Basic Trainer (Tachikawa Ki-17) and the Type 95 Medium Trainer (Tachikawa Ki-9). Over a six-month period trainees would receive up to 70 hours of dual instruction and solo flying.

Moving to advanced flying training schools (Kyoiku Hikotai), trainees would begin flying the Type 99 Advanced Trainer (Tachikawa Ki-55). At this stage they would practice formation flying, more aerobatics and elementary combat tactics. Those selected to become fighter pilots would move on to fly obsolescent operational aircraft such as the Type 97 Fighter (Ki-27) and Type 1 Fighter (Ki-43). During his advanced training a trainee

Tachikawa Type 95 trainers at the Kōku Shikan Gakkō (Army Air Academy), which trained officer pilots, prepare for takeoff. Officer pilots underwent a separate training program from enlisted aviators. (Author's collection)

pilot would receive 120 hours of dual instruction and solo flying over six to eight months.

From an advanced flying training school a pilot moved to an operational fighter regiment for operational training. Ideally, over six months, the neophyte fighter pilot would receive an additional 200 to 300 hours of training in combat tactics and gunnery from experienced combat pilots, usually when a unit had been withdrawn from the front line for rest and re-equipment.

Although the JAAF's training organization was expanded during 1941–42, it still could not produce the number of fighter pilots needed to replace growing losses in combat. Nor could the system of operational training at unit level function well as Hikō Sentai increasingly remained in combat for extended periods. This meant that new pilots were often thrown into combat before completing their training. To provide more pilots for the JAAF and IJNAF, the Japanese government authorized the

The Tachikawa Type 99 Advanced Trainer (Ki-55 "Ida") acted as a bridge between the Ki-9 and the more demanding operational fighter aircraft a young pilot would fly in his last stage of training. This photograph shows Ki-55s from the Kōku Shikan Gakkō (Army Air Academy) practicing formation flying. (Author's collection)

WILLIAM SNIDER

Capt William Snider of VMF-221 claimed two "Franks" shot down over Kyushu on March 18, 1945, and his wingman claimed a third. Another division of VMF-221 claimed two more during the same mission. (RG-80, 80-G-259865, NARA)

William Snider is representative of the experienced US Navy and US Marine Corps division leaders who fought during the final months of the Pacific War. Snider was born in December 1918 in Cairo, Illinois. He appears to have entered US Navy flying training before Pearl Harbor, receiving his commission as a second lieutnant in the US Marine Corps on May 22, 1942. In December he reported to VMF-221, stationed in Hawaii. Equipped with the F4F-4 Wildcat, the squadron was shipped to the Solomon Islands in February 1943, arriving on Guadalcanal in March. It would fly two combat tours from Guadalcanal, and a third tour based at Vella Lavella. On April 1, 1943, VMF-221 had its first encounter with Japanese aircraft, claiming seven shot down over the Russell Islands. 1Lt William Snider claimed three Zero-sens destroyed in his F4F-4 in the space of just 90 seconds.

VMF-221 converted to the F4U-1 Corsair in May, but Snider did not score again until October 17, when he claimed two "Zekes" shot down and a third probably destroyed over Bougainville, making him an ace. Snider received a Distinguished Flying Cross and an Air Medal for his actions on his first combat tour, duly being promoted to captain. VMF-221 returned to the USA in January 1944. Snider remained with the squadron, helping to train new pilots as the unit prepared for its second combat tour. Combat-experienced pilots like Snider were instrumental in passing on tactics and helping replacements hone their combat skills.

At the end of the year VMF-221 was chosen as one of the US Marine Corps Corsair squadrons to be assigned to a fleet carrier, joining VMF-451 in Carrier Air Group 84 assigned to USS *Bunker Hill* (CV-17). Snider made the first claim of his second combat tour on February 16, 1945 during TF 58's strike on Tokyo when he and a squadronmate shot down a G4M "Betty" bomber. A month later Snider participated in the carrier strikes on airfields on Kyushu, claiming two "Franks" and a "Zeke" shot down in an intense aerial battle. For this action he was awarded the Silver Star.

Snider claimed a "Tony" shot down on April 6 during the Kikusui Operation No 1. Ten days later he was credited with destroying a "Tojo" and a "Zeke" during Kikusui Operation No 3, but there is a possibility that the Ki-44 he claimed was actually a "Frank" from the 35th Sei – a Special Attack unit operating from Formosa that day. This would make Snider one of the leading US Navy and US Marine Corps scorers against the Type 4 Fighter. These were Snider's final claims of the war, bringing his total to 11.5 Japanese aircraft destroyed. On May 11 *Bunker Hill* was severely damaged in a kamikaze attack, after which Snider and the other surviving pilots of VMF-221 returned home and saw no further combat. Snider left the US Marine Corps after the war and died in March 1969.

KATSUAKI KIRA

By 1945 JAAF pilots with WO Kira's experience were all too rare. Born in Kumamoto Prefecture, on the island of Kyushu, in 1919, he completed his military and flight training in July 1938 and was transferred to the Akeno Army Flying School, where he trained as a fighter pilot. Promoted to corporal (prior to 1941, two-thirds of JAAF pilots were enlisted men), Kira joined the 24th Hikō Sentai in northeast China. He had his first experience of combat flying the Type 97 Fighter (Ki-27 "Nate") during the Nomonhan Incident of 1939, claiming nine victories against Soviet aircraft between June and September of that year.

Kira participated in the invasion of the Philippines with the 24th Hikō Sentai but did not claim any victories. In September 1942 the unit transferred to Sumatra, where it converted to the Type 1 Fighter (Ki-43 "Oscar"). From there, the 24th Hikō Sentai went to New Guinea in May 1943. Kira spent six months in-theater, claiming seven victories against American airplanes, including a B-17 and a B-24.

The Sentai returned to Japan in October 1943, and that same month Kira was assigned to the new 200th Hikō Sentai, made up of instructors from the Akeno Army Flying School flying the new Ki-84. He fought throughout the Philippines campaign, scoring several more victories. On one mission Kira attacked a formation of P-38s, claiming two shot down. For this feat he received a promotion to warrant officer. Returning to Japan, Kira was assigned to the 103rd Hikō Sentai in March 1945 and participated in air combat over Okinawa, scoring the last of his 21 victories during the fighting. He survived six years of aerial combat over China, New Guinea, the Philippines and Okinawa – a remarkable achievement that not many equaled. After the war Kira joined the Japanese Self-Defense Force, retiring as a major.

Ace WO Katsuaki Kira survived six years of aerial combat over China, New Guinea, the Philippines and Okinawa, having progress from Ki-27s to Ki-84s during his remarkably long career in the front line. (Courtesy Yasuho Izawa)

[Source – United States Strategic Bombing Survey: *Japanese Air Power*]

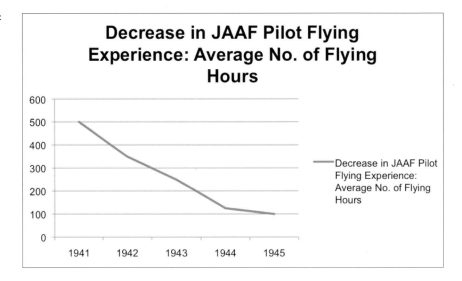

Decrease in JAAF Pilot Flying Experience: Average No. of Flying Hours

Decrease in JAAF Pilot Flying Experience: Average No. of Flying Hours

conscription of university and secondary school students in the fall of 1943. To cope with this influx of pilot trainees, the JAAF increased the number of Kyoiku Hikotai from 18 to 50 in the spring of 1944, establishing many of these new units overseas in China, Korea, Manchuria, Malaya, French Indochina and Java so that they were closer to supplies of aviation fuel.

At the same time, the JAAF removed the training burden from operational units and created specialized operational training units (Rensei Hikotai), which were placed overseas as well as in the Home Islands. Instructors for the Rensei Hikotai were drawn from the advanced training schools and from experienced pilots who had been withdrawn from combat, often after being badly wounded. The Rensei Hikotai were equipped with operational aircraft, including the Type 1, Type 2, Type 3 and Type 4 Fighters. These units were made responsible for converting graduates of the advanced flying training schools to the operational aircraft they would fly in combat and teaching them combat techniques, in addition to conversion training for experienced pilots. In some cases the Rensei Hikotai provided local air defense and flew convoy patrols to relieve regular fighter regiments of these duties, providing a supplement to operational training.

The rapid expansion of pilot trainees created problems because of a shortage of training aircraft and instructor pilots. These shortages led to disruptions and delays in the training program. The more critical factor was the growing shortage of aviation fuel as US Navy submarines sank more and more Japanese tankers. The influx of trainees at the same time that fuel supplies were dwindling meant fewer training hours per trainee. The shortage of fuel forced the JAAF to cut back pilot training to nine months during 1944, and to four months in early 1945. Whereas pilots previously would have accumulated 400 to 500 hours of flying time before entering combat, by early 1944 the average had dropped to around 300 hours, and it continued to decline as the year went on. With fewer flying hours allocated to them, JAAF pilot trainees had less and less chance to build their fundamental flying skills and obtain the experience they would need for air combat. Training in combat tactics and gunnery had to be cut back too.

With the expectation of American bombing raids from the Mariana Islands, from the fall of 1944 much of the operational training new pilots received was devoted to intercepting bomber formations at high altitude, and less time was allocated to fighter-versus-fighter combat beyond some basic fighter maneuvers.

For a newly trained fighter pilot, however, the Type 4 Fighter's flying characteristics were considered to be superior to other JAAF fighters. Conversion to the Type 4 was thought to be straightforward, although neophyte pilots did have problems landing the more powerful fighter. The Ki-84 was not as instantly maneuverable as the Type 1 Fighter, but its heavier weight and heavier control response made it easier to fly. It had superior handling to the Type 2 Fighter, which some experienced pilots considered to be "twitchy and unstable," especially at higher altitude, and benefited from a lower landing speed than the Type 2. Commenting on converting from the Type 2 to the Type 4 Fighter, a pilot from the 47th Hikō Sentai recalled, "the hachi-yon [Ki-84] was much easier to control than the yon-yon [Ki-44], which had a higher landing speed. It only took me a few days to get used to it since the changeover. Everyone said it was an easy airplane to fly."

But while learning to fly the Ki-84 was straightforward, as with their IJNAF counterparts, fewer and fewer JAAF fighter pilots trained in the final year of the war had the skills to get the most out of their new fighter, as good as it was.

At a Rensei Hikotai or another Army Flying School, neophyte fighter pilots would fly their first operational fighters, beginning with the Type 97 Fighter (Ki-27 "Nate") or the Type 1 Fighter (Ki-43 "Oscar"), shown here, before moving on to the more demanding Type 2 Fighter (Ki-44 "Tojo") and the Type 4 Fighter (Ki-84 "Frank"). (Peter M. Bowers Collection, Museum of Flight)

COMBAT

US NAVY AND US MARINE CORPS COMBAT TACTICS

Through hard-won experience, the US Navy had refined its basic fighter combat tactics to four key principles:

- Superiority of Position
- Superiority of Disposition
- Superiority of Concentration
- Superiority of Marksmanship

Superiority of position referred to the necessity of maintaining superior altitude over enemy aircraft and staying between an enemy force and its objective, while superiority of disposition spoke to arranging formations so that all sections and divisions could be employed efficiently. Superiority of concentration was perhaps the most important element in fighter combat – the vital necessity of pilots keeping together to maintain air discipline and mutual protection. The US Navy stressed over and over the need for mutual support and coordinated action. Its combat doctrine clearly stated that "each airplane is part of an invisible chain. Any airplane which breaks the chain by diving away, either to avoid an enemy or in pursuit of a target, subtracts from the overall strength of the group." If fighters remained concentrated, and fought together as a team, "they will command the air where they are concentrated."

The division of four aircraft, in two elements, was the basic combat formation for the US Navy and US Marine Corps fighter units. Pilots were drilled to fight as a team both offensively and defensively, and admonished never to break off to engage in combat on their own. A division of four Corsairs from VBF-84 are shown here flying in formation in the final months of the Pacific War. (Robert Lawson Collection, National Naval Aviation Museum)

Superiority of marksmanship was itself based on four principles:

- Ability to hit with the first burst.
- Ability to make effective runs in the heat of battle on maneuvering targets.
- Cool selection of the point of aim – engine, pilot or tanks, rather than spraying the whole target.
- Conservation of ammunition.

Beginning in intermediate training, and continuing through operational training and initial squadron service, these principles were drummed into new fighter pilots. From a trainee pilot's first gunnery runs to his introduction to combat, the US Navy and the US Marine Corps stressed the importance of marksmanship and the fundamentals of aerial gunnery. As the US Navy's gunnery manual put it, "the intelligent combat pilot knows his responsibilities and he strives for perfection in fundamentals in order to achieve a cool, smooth, machine-like precision in action. He corrects his mistakes in practice, for in actual combat the smallest individual error may cause the loss of a battle."

Superiority of position, disposition, concentration and marksmanship were vital in defending against the kamikaze attacks during the Okinawa campaign. To protect the carrier task force and the many transports bringing supplies for the ground battle, US Navy and US Marine Corps fighter squadrons spent hours on CAPs under fighter direction from controllers onboard radar picket ships or manning land-based portable radar stations. Successful interceptions required

This photograph of a "Zeke" under attack during the Philippines campaign illustrates several principles of US Navy combat tactics. The naval aviator is attacking from behind with an altitude advantage (superiority of position) and appears to be selecting the "Zeke's" wing tanks as his target (superiority of marksmanship). (RG80, 80-G-46984, NARA)

CAPs were usually under the direction of a Fighter Director Officer. Fighters would stay closed up in one of four formations as they approached the intercept point to avoid confusing the radar. The formations were designed to place the main intercepting force some 2,000–3,000ft above the estimated height of the enemy formation to give superiority of position, with a part of the formation flying above to provide high cover. Formations varied based on visibility and the probable composition of the enemy formation.

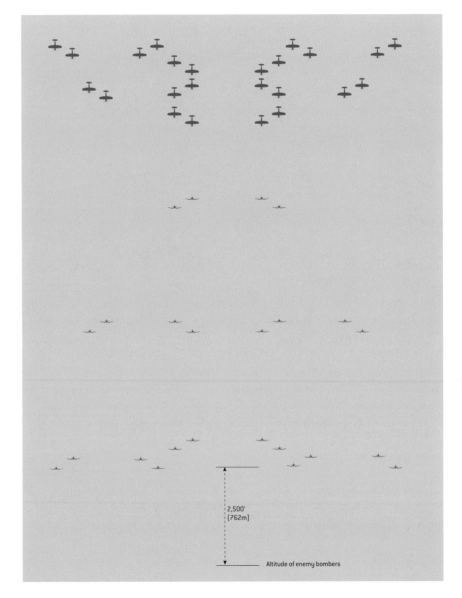

2,500'
(762m)

Altitude of enemy bombers

excellent cooperation between fighter squadrons and the Fighter Direction Officer who directed the intercept.

Approaching the intercept point, fighters would shift to one of four formations – designated "Victor," "William," "X-ray" or "Yoke" – depending on visibility, the accuracy of the estimated altitude of the enemy formation and whether or not it was escorted. These formations would attempt to bring the fighters in at an altitude above the enemy formation, with the flight leader's division flying above other divisions to ensure accurate direction of the engagement. The flight leader would deploy his divisions to obtain superiority of disposition and concentration, always trying to attack with an altitude advantage and, if possible, to engage escorting fighters while other divisions went after the Special Attack airplanes, although it appears that identifying escorts from Special Attack airplanes was not always straightforward.

It was accepted that in an attack the principle of concentration might have to be violated, but doctrine stressed the importance of maintaining tactical concentration at the section and, if possible, division level. Pilots were admonished not to break away from their leader to engage an enemy airplane, as mutual support would break down, leaving one or both airplanes unprotected. The US Navy wanted an "organized melee" instead of a general "melee," where there was greater risk. Doctrine stated that in attacking a large formation of enemy aircraft "success will depend largely on the ability of pilots to follow the leader, maintain effective tactical concentration, preventing straggling and the pursuit of individual enemy airplanes."

JAAF COMBAT TACTICS

During the Pacific War, JAAF air combat tactics evolved as commanders came to recognize that they were less effective against an enemy employing coordinated formations and air discipline, airplanes with superior performance and well-trained pilots. In the years leading up to the Pacific War, and in the conflict's early stages, JAAF fighter pilots were obsessed with maneuverability. They retained the belief that air combat would continue to be a battle between two combatants in a whirling, turning dogfight, with the aircraft with superior maneuverability inevitably the victor. Japanese pilots believed that a light armament of two 7.7mm machine guns was adequate because of their ability to place their fighter in an advantageous position for a "single-shot" that resulted in the "certain death" of an enemy pilot.

The Type 97 Fighter exemplified this approach to close-in air combat and the emphasis on agility above all other characteristics. The Type 1 Fighter made a concession to the trend toward heavier fighter armament by switching to two 12.7mm machine guns, but retained the emphasis on maneuvering into a superior position for the kill.

JAAF fighter tactics in the first part of the war aimed at drawing an opponent into maneuvering combat, where the superior agility of Japanese aircraft could be brought

JAAF pilots receive a briefing from their commanding officer before heading off on a mission. Once in the air, the poor quality of Japanese aerial radios made communications between a leader and his formation difficult. (Author's collection)

Three young JAAF enlisted pilots pose for a photograph. By early 1945 pilot training had been cut back to the extent that young pilots were joining their units with around 200 flying hours and only the most basic training in aerial combat. (Author's collection)

to bear. Like their IJNAF counterparts, JAAF regiments used the three-airplane Shotai as their basic formation, although this was a more fluid scheme than the standard V formation of most other air forces. The No 2 and No 3 pilots in the Shotai were not rigidly attached to the Shotai leader, but had more flexibility in maneuver. In an attack, the No 2 and No 3 pilots often followed their leader in when engaging an enemy airplane, or lagged behind to catch an enemy fighter as it tried to maneuver away from the leader's attack.

When attacked from behind, a Shotai formation would often split up, the leader pulling up in a loop to use superior maneuverability to come down behind an Allied fighter, while the No 2 and No 3 pilots executed a chandelle or an Immelmann turn to gain an advantageous position to counter the attack. These tactics proved highly effective in the early months of the Pacific War before Allied pilots learned to avoid maneuvering combat with the more nimble Japanese fighters and adopted dive-and-zoom, hit-and-run tactics instead. Using their superior speed and diving ability, Allied pilots could initiate an attack from higher altitude, then break away and climb back above a Japanese formation to launch another attack. In their lighter and slower aircraft, Japanese pilots found these tactics difficult to counter.

During 1943 JAAF air leaders recognized the need to revise fighter tactics. They conducted extensive research, drawing on their experiences of combat with Allied fighter pilots and their knowledge of German combat tactics. A report issued toward the end of the year brought out the need for greater air discipline and mutual support.

In combat, the JAAF had found that the three-airplane Shotai formation proved difficult to coordinate and provided weaker protection. Training had emphasized individual over coordinated action in combat. Once engaged with an enemy formation, JAAF fighter pilots had a tendency to conduct individual attacks, with little thought given to mutual support. Often, the formation broke up into one- and two-airplane groupings, leaving the single fighter isolated and vulnerable to attack.

Following German and Allied practice, the JAAF belatedly switched to a two-airplane element as its basic combat formation, increasing the Shotai to four airplanes in two sections (Buntai) of two airplanes for greater mutual support. There was also a greater emphasis on seeking a more advantageous position prior to engaging in combat, especially the need to attack with an altitude advantage as the Allies did. Pilots were admonished not to engage in combat on their own.

In aerial combat over Japan and Okinawa during 1945, US Navy and US Marine Corps pilots noted an improvement in Japanese tactics. Pilots would climb for altitude before attacking, and would try to maintain an altitude advantage. They would attack

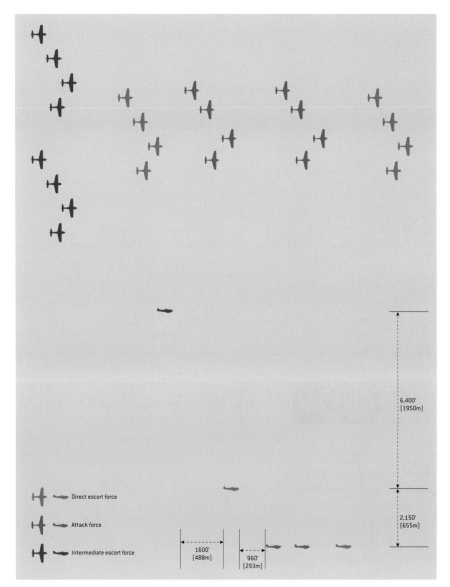

The escorts had three objectives to fulfill when protecting the Special Attack unit formations. Because so many of the kamikaze pilots were inexperienced, the escorts would guide them to their targets. The direct escort force would fly alongside or among the Special Attack aircraft as guides. The intermediate escort force and the direct escort force would attempt to clear a path for the Special Attack aircraft through the American CAPs. Assuming the Special Attack aircraft made it through to their targets, the escort force was instructed to observe and report on the results achieved, before returning to base.

when there was an opportunity – a wingman out of formation, a pilot straggling after a low-altitude strafing run, or a pilot who went too far out in a weave. However, effective use of the two-airplane element and four-airplane formation did not appear to be the case in all JAAF fighter units. US Navy and US Marine Corps pilots continued to comment on the failure of their Japanese foes to provide mutual support.

A great handicap to improved air discipline and formation tactics was the poor quality of Japanese airborne radios. It was often difficult, and sometimes impossible, for a formation leader to maintain voice contact with the pilots in the formation. This problem was never satisfactorily addressed before the end of the Pacific War. A pilot who flew the Type 5 Fighter (Ki-100) late in the conflict recalled the problems poor radios caused. "The aeroplane's radio equipment was very poor," he remembered. "This defect was common to all Japanese aircraft. I had heard that the enemy airplanes

During 1944, the Japanese government began conscripting university and high school students to train as pilots. Since many of these classes would not complete their training before the likely invasion of the homeland, large numbers of students were trained as kamikaze pilots for the Tōkubetsu Kogeki Tai (Special Attack Units). (Author's collection)

had very good communications equipment, and that they had no difficulty in calling for reinforcements while in combat. In the case of Japanese airplanes, radio communications were of no use, and no plane came to our assistance on such occasions."

The switch to the four-airplane formation and hit-and-run tactics toward the end of 1943 and early 1944 coincided with the introduction of the Type 4 Fighter into the JAAF's frontline regiments. The Type 4 Fighter was ideally suited to the newer hit-and-run tactics. Heavier, sturdier and faster in the dive than the Type 1 Fighter, with more power at altitude and maneuverablity than the Type 2 Fighter, the Hayate had the ability to dive down on American fighter formations at speed, fire a burst from its machine guns and cannon and climb back to altitude with a rate of climb superior to the F4U Corsair, F6F Hellcat, P-47 Thunderbolt or P-51 Mustang. And if the combat broke up into a turning fight, the Hayate was more maneuverable than the American fighters and could execute the standard split-S evasive maneuver more readily.

The Type 4 Fighter gave its pilots confidence. An aviator who flew the Hayate with the 47th Hikō Sentai in the defense of Japan towards the end of the war recalled that he went into combat thinking "it will work out as long as the battle is fought one-on-one, and the skills and conditions of the enemy pilot were equivalent. I thought the Hachi-yon was superior."

The difficulty for the Type 4 Fighter sentai in these final aerial battles of the war was that on many of the missions they flew the Hayates were mostly on the defensive. Hit-and-run tactics required altitude, and gaining sufficient altitude for the defense of the airfields on Kyushu required adequate warning, which did not always happen. As one Hayate pilot put it, "if the battle was fighter against fighter, usually the one who had the higher position won. When you take off into skies where the enemy is waiting, you might as well take off into Hell." In some units at least, one chutai (squadron) would be assigned to fly cover over the airfield to protect the other squadrons as they took off to intercept and returned for landing.

While escorting the kamikaze formations to Okinawa, the Type 4 Fighter Sentais often found themselves at a disadvantage, tied to the Special Attack formations. The escort force usually flew in two types of formation – direct and intermediate escort. The direct escort force would either fly intermixed with the Special Attack airplanes, acting as guide aircraft, or as a separate force flying ahead and behind the Special Attack force, with the rear escorts flying slightly above. The intermediate escort force would fly above and behind the direct escort and Special Attack airplanes to give them room to maneuver against attacking American fighters.

FIRST ENCOUNTERS

Following the fall of the Philippines, Imperial General Headquarters began preparations for the defense of the Home Islands against an expected American invasion, likely to begin with an attack on the Ryukyu Islands to establish a base for air support of the invasion force. On January 20, 1945, Imperial General Headquarters issued an outline of JAAF and IJNAF operations, a key component of which was a joint plan for the air defense of the Ryukyus and the Homeland. Given shortages of more capable airplanes, fuel and especially experienced pilots, the emphasis in the air plan was the mass employment of Special Attack units, the Tōkubetsu Kogeki Tai (also called Shimbu Tai, Special Attack Units, known to Americans as the kamikaze), using partly trained pilots and, in the main, obsolete aircraft.

A Corsair from VF-84 prepares to take off from *Bunker Hill* on one of the early Tokyo strikes in February 1945. Some squadrons used a yellow ring around the cowling as a recognition feature. (RG-80, 80-G-310075, NARA)

In December 1944 the JAAF had established the 6th Kōkūgun (6th Air Army) as a reserve force to counter the planned invasion of the Ryukyus and the Home Islands, operating both regular and Special Attack units. With the invasion of Okinawa, the 6th Kōkūgun became responsible for conducting Special Attack missions under Operation *"Ten-Go"*, the defense of Okinawa, and for protecting the JAAF's airfields on Kyushu, operating under the control of the IJNAF's Rengō Kantai (Combined Fleet). The JAAF's contribution to the air defense of the Home Islands remained with the 1st Kōkūgun, with its 10th, 11th and 12th Hikōshidan (10th, 11th and 12th Air Divisions).

The Type 4 Hayate served with fighter sentai in both air armies. In general, the Hayate units serving with the 1st Kōkūgun were responsible for the air defense of Japan's industrial areas against attacks from B-29 bombers and American carrier aircraft. The 6th Kōkūgun's Hayate units had responsibility for defending the Special Attack unit airfields on Kyushu from marauding US Navy carrier aircraft, as well as being given the unenviable task of escorting the Tōkubetsu Tai on their missions to attack American shipping off Okinawa. Although most of the JAAF's Shimbu Tai units were equipped with obsolete Type 97 (Ki-27) and Type 1 (Ki-43) fighters, Type 99 Assault airplanes (Ki-51) and training aircraft, a few units were assigned Type 3 (Ki-61) and Type 4 fighters for their Special Attack missions.

US Navy and US Marine Corps Corsair pilots flying off carriers or from airfields on Okinawa would encounter the Type 4 fighter in all three roles during the initial carrier strikes against the Home Islands, throughout the Okinawa campaign and in the final few combats of the last months of the Pacific War.

One difficulty in looking at engagements between the Corsair and the Hayate is the problem of aircraft recognition. The speed and intensity of aerial combat, often against large formations of different types of Japanese aircraft, made it difficult to positively identify the airplane being attacked. During this late-war period the JAAF fielded four radial-engined fighters – the Type 1 Hayabusa (Ki-43 "Oscar"), Type 2 Shoki (Ki-44 "Tojo"), Type 4 Hayate (Ki-84 "Frank") and the Type 5 (Ki-100, which

During February 1945 the fast carriers of TF 58 launched a series of strikes against airfields and aircraft factories in the Tokyo region. The carrier airplanes struck on February 16, and returned the next day, but poor weather and Japanese interceptors limited the effectiveness of the attacks. After covering the invasion of Iwo Jima, TF 58 returned to strike the Tokyo area again on February 25. That morning Lt Cdr Roger Hedrick, CO of VF-84 flying off *Bunker Hill*, was leading four divisions on a fighter sweep east of Tokyo. Hedrick was an experienced Corsair pilot, having flown F4Us with VF-17 in the Solomons, where he claimed nine "Zekes" shot down. In poor weather, with a solid overcast above, Hedrick spotted eight Japanese fighters he identified as "Franks" circling over an airfield below his flight level, with two more "Franks" flying beneath the Japanese formation. He dove down with his division and came in behind a "Frank" at the "seven o'clock" position, firing and getting hits in the wing roots and the fuselage. The Japanese fighter started burning and went down. On his second pass against the Japanese formation Hedrick came in directly behind another "Frank" and opened fire from close range, again getting hits in the wing root and fuselage. This "Frank" exploded. Hedrick's wingman, Ens Thomas Mitchell claimed a third "Frank", while his element leader, Lt William Gerner claimed a probable and a damaged. The Corsairs demonstrated superior speed to their opponents at this low altitude. The Japanese pilots appeared to lack aggressiveness, which Hedrick attributed to poor training or lack of combat experience.

had no Allied code name). The IJNAF fielded three – the A6M Zero-sen ("Zeke"), the J2M Raiden ("Jack") and the N1K2-J Shiden-Kai ("George").

For many Allied pilots the "Frank" was a relatively new airplane that few would have seen before. While it had gone into combat during the late summer of 1944 over China and Burma, it was not until the Philippines campaign in October of that same year that US Navy pilots encountered the "Frank" in any significant numbers, and not until US forces captured several examples that the fighter's features and outlines could be clearly defined. As a Technical Air Intelligence Center report on the Type 4 from January 1945 noted, the "Frank 1 does definitely resemble both Oscar 2 and Tojo 2. The wing structure is similar to that of Oscar and the fuselage and tailplane closely resemble Tojo."

It is not surprising, therefore, that US Navy and US Marine Corps pilots often mistook "Franks" for the more familiar "Tojos," although during the Okinawa battles the Ki-44 units were in fact committed to air defense over Japan, or mistook "Franks" for "Georges" because of their superior performance, or saw any brown-coloured Japanese fighter airplane as an "Oscar" or a "Zeke." Understandably these young fighter pilots had more on their minds than properly identifying the airplane they were shooting at. Therefore, Aircraft Action Reports have to be approached with a degree of caution. It is sometimes possible to link combats between American Corsair units and Japanese Hayate units, but not in every case.

As no US Marine Corps Corsair unit claimed a "Frank" over the Philippines, and the US Navy Corsair units were not involved in that campaign, the first apparent clash between F4Us and Ki-84s took place on February 25, 1945 during the carrier strikes TF 58 had launched against airfields and aircraft factories in the Tokyo area in support of the landings on Iwo Jima. Flying off USS *Bunker Hill* (CV-17), Lt Cdr Roger Hedrick, commander of VF-84, was leading 16 F4U-1D Corsairs on a morning fighter sweep over airfields east of Tokyo.

On the first two days of attacks on February 16 and 17, JAAF and IJNAF interceptors rose up in force to challenge the American airplanes, the Type 4 pilots of the 47th Hikō Sentai claiming 14 F6F Hellcats shot down and US Navy pilots submitting claims for six "Franks" destroyed in return.

On the 25th the weather was overcast at 5,000ft, with snow falling over some areas, limiting interceptions. Hedrick was an experienced fighter pilot, having claimed nine "Zekes" destroyed in F4Us with shore-based VF-17 in the Solomons. Flying at the base of the overcast, the Corsairs spotted eight Japanese aircraft they identified as "Franks" flying below them, with two more "Franks" flying below and ahead of the Japanese formation. Leaving two divisions as top cover, Hedrick came down on one of the "Franks," closing in and firing from the "seven o'clock" position. He hit the fighter in the fuselage and wing roots, sending the airplane down on fire. His wingman, Ens Thomas Mitchell, claimed another "Frank" in the same pass. Lt William Gerner fired at a third "Frank," but could not get it to burn – it went down smoking and was credited as damaged. Hedrick made a second pass on the formation, claiming another "Frank" shot down from directly astern.

The Corsair pilots were then jumped by a mixed formation they identified as "Oscars," "Zekes" and "Franks." Gerner fired on another "Frank," getting hits and sending the airplane down smoking and seemingly out of control. The VF-84 pilots noted that the Japanese fighters appeared to have a high "rate of zoom," pulling

quickly up into the overcast to avoid combat in a lack of aggressiveness that Hedrick contributed to poor training or inexperience. These airplanes, if they were indeed Hayates, were likely from the 47th Hikō Sentai, based nearby.

A month later, on March 18, carrier-based Corsair squadron VMF-221, also flying off *Bunker Hill*, ran into a formation its pilots identified as "Franks" and "Zekes" while on a fighter sweep over central Kyushu as part of TF 58's strikes against airfields in the area. Here, too, there is a question about aircraft identification, as in the normal course of operations JAAF and IJNAF squadrons rarely flew together. However, on this day, both JAAF and IJNAF fighters were scrambled in an effort to counter the American raids. The 6th Kōkūgun had on Kyushu the 100th Hikōdan (Air Brigade) with the 101st, 102nd and 103rd Hikō Sentai equipped with the Type 4 fighter. The "Franks" VMF-221 encountered may have been from one of these units.

Three divisions of Corsairs from VMF-221 attacked an aircraft factory at Kumamoto, in central Kyushu, on the 18th. After expending their rockets on buildings, the F4U pilots were heading east towards the coast when they ran into a formation of 25 Japanese fighters. Captain William Snider, leading a division, attacked at once, firing at a fighter he identified as a "Frank" approaching him head-on from "11 o'clock level." Snider was an experienced pilot on his second combat tour, having

claimed six "Zekes" over the Solomons flying Wildcats and Corsairs. Snider continued firing until nearly colliding with the "Frank," setting it on fire. He then attacked a second "Frank" from above, coming in from the "seven o'clock" position. He set this "Frank" on fire too, the pilot bailing out. Snider's wingman, 1Lt Donald McFarlane, claimed a third "Frank" shot down, while 1Lt Neylon Murphy was credited with two damaged. In the third division, 1Lt Joseph Brocia Jr and 2Lt Richard Wasley both claimed "Franks" shot down.

In what had been only a short combat, three VMF-221 divisions claimed eight "Zekes" and five "Franks" shot down. In the Aircraft Action Report the pilots observed that "'Franks' and 'Zekes' did not use their natural advantages to any extent – even their turns were wide and sloppy. Their speed and dives were inferior, and their only maneuver seemed to be the split-S. The 'Franks' seemed to absorb more lead than the 'Zekes' and be harder to burn. Both types executed head-on attacks, however."

What emerges from these two early actions is a paradox that would be repeated in the majority of combats between the Corsair and the Hayate in the months to come. Here was a fighter airplane with significant performance, armament capable of engaging American fighters in head-on attacks and improved armor protection, the latter making the Ki-84 much harder to set on fire than earlier Japanese fighters like the "Oscar" and the "Zeke." Yet many of the Japanese pilots flying the Hayate seemed incapable, through lack of training or experience, of getting the best out of their fighters and using their capabilities to their advantage. For those pilots designated for Special Attack missions, the options for using their fighters to their full potential were limited.

OKINAWA CAMPAIGN

The JAAF and IJNAF air plan for Operation *"Ten-Go"* was to launch ten mass kamikaze attacks against the American invasion force off Okinawa and the fleet units of TF 58. These attacks, dubbed Kikusui, began with Kikusui Operation No 1 on April 6, 1945 and continued until the last attack, Kikusui Operation No 10, on June 21-22 1945. Spread over one to three days, the strikes involved Special Attack units

The JAAF established several Shimbu-Tai units equipped with the Type 4 Fighter. The Ki-84s carried a 250kg bomb under one wing and a drop tank under the other. Some of the escorting fighters would also carry a bomb for conventional attacks. (Courtesy Philip Jarrett)

from both the JAAF and the IJNAF. The former had gathered its remaining experienced pilots into regular fighter regiments to act as escorts for the Special Attack units, hopefully clearing a path to enemy ships through the CAPs.

Although most of the Special Attack aircraft were obsolete fighter and trainer types, the JAAF did assign more capable Type 3 Hien (Ki-61 "Tony") and Type 4 Hayate to some of the Special Attack units. During the Okinawa campaign, for example, the Type 4 fighter equipped the 26th, 57th, 58th, 59th, 60th and 61st Shimbu-Tai units flying out of Kyushu and the 33rd, 34th, 35th and 120th Sei squadrons based on Formosa. The three Hayate Sentai of the 100th Hikōshidan (101st, 102nd and 103rd) regularly flew as escort. The losses suffered by the 100th Hikōshidan's units were considerable – during the aerial battles over the Homeland and Okinawa in 1945 the three Sentai lost more than 70 pilots in combat.

Following the invasion of Okinawa on April 1, 1945, carrier-based US Navy and US Marine Corps Corsair squadrons (VF-5, VF-10, VBF-10, VBF-83, VF-84, VF-85 and VMF-112, VMF-123, VMF-221 and VMF-451) flew regular CAPs over US Navy shipping in the anchorages off Okinawa and over TF 58. Land-based Corsair units began flying CAPs on April 7 when MAG-31 arrived at Yontan airfield, on Okinawa, with VMF-224, VMF-311 and VMF-441. Two days later MAG-33 began operating from Kadena airfield, also on Okinawa, with VMF-312, VMF-322 and VMF-323 (MAG-22, with VMF-113, VMF-314 and VMF-422, arrived in May and MAG-14, with VMF-212, VMF-222 and VMF-223, equipped with the newer F4U-4 Corsair arrived in June).

During the series of Kikusui attacks these squadrons intercepted many formations of different types of Special Attack aircraft, and their escorts, attempting to sink US Navy transports or the all-important radar picket ships off Okinawa. Formations of Type 4 Fighters were included in this number.

Again, the problem of aircraft recognition makes it difficult to determine with any degree of precision exactly which combats were between Corsairs and "Franks," and how many of either type were shot down by the other. In some cases US Navy and US Marine Corps pilots would identify "Franks" as their opponents, but often claims for "Franks" would be mixed with other types, notably "Tojos," "Oscars" or "Zekes." Since none of the Shimbu-Tai units was equipped with the Ki-44, it is probable that many,

Aircraft from one of MAG-33's three Corsair squadrons take off from Kadena field on Okinawa in April 1945. MAG-31 operated three Corsair squadrons from nearby Yontan field. (RG 127, 127-GW-119276, NARA)

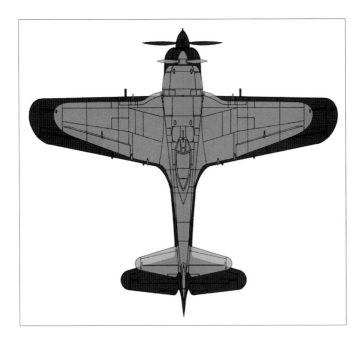

This artwork shows the outline of a Ki-44 "Tojo" laid over the outline of a Ki-84 "Frank" to illustrate the problem of aircraft recognition. In the aerial battles around Okinawa, US Navy and US Marine Corps pilots appear to have often mistaken the "Frank" for the more familiar "Tojo". It seems that no Ki-44s were used as either Special Attack aircraft or as escorts for Shimbu-Tai units heading for Okinawa. (Illustration courtesy P. J. Muller, Museum of Flight)

but not all, of these combats where US Navy and US Marine Corps pilots claimed "Tojos" actually involved the "Frank." The dates on which US Navy and US Marine Corps Corsair squadrons claimed "Franks" and "Tojos" do correspond fairly closely with the dates on which the Shimbu-Tai units equipped with the Type 4 Fighter were active, and they usually had Ki-84s from the regular fighter Sentais as escort.

The first of these combats with multiple Ki-84-equipped Shimbu-Tai units took place on April 28 during Kikusui Operation No 4, when VF-84 claimed four "Franks" and one "Tojo.. That day, the 61st Shimbu-Tai unit sent seven Ki-84s to attack shipping west of Okinawa, as did several Shimbu-Tai units equipped with Type 97 Fighters, with an escort of Ki-84s from the 101st Hikō Sentai, which lost two fighters that day. VF-84 had four divisions on CAP, and after spotting the Japanese formation they attacked it from above and behind. Lieutenant (jg) Cyrus Chambers claimed two "Franks" shot down, while Lt(jg)s Willard Rempel and Harvey Matthews were credited with one each. Lieutenant (jg) R. E. Miller claimed a "Tojo," which was no doubt a "Frank," noting that it took five bursts to shoot down the Japanese fighter.

On May 4 pilots of VF-84 claimed a further three "Franks" shot down during Kikusui Operation No 5. The Corsairs of VBF-83 also ran into several Ki-84s, Ens Roy Rechsteiner claiming two shot down. He also noted that neither of his opponents carried any bombs, indicating that they were possibly part of the escort force. That day the 60th Shimbu-Tai unit sent out six Ki-84s to attack shipping, while the 36th and 120th Sei squadrons from Formosa dispatched nine Ki-84s to Okinawa. Several hours later a pilot from VMF-323 claimed a "Tojo" during a combat with a large force of Special Attack aircraft. On May 7 VMF-323 claimed two "Tojos" shot down, with VBF-83 being credited with a third. It is possible that these were in fact "Franks," not "Tojos."

The greatest number of claims came on May 25 during Kikusui Operation No 7. On this day the JAAF sent 100 Special Attack aircraft to Okinawa, including 23 Ki-84s from the 26th, 57th, 58th, 60th and 61st Shimbu-Tai. The 102nd Hikō Sentai, and possibly other units of the 100th Hikōshidan, flew as escort, the 102nd losing at least two pilots that day. The Corsairs of VMF-312 appear to have been the first to run into these formations. Captain Herbert Valentine's division, having just been relieved from their CAP, saw a formation of what they identified as 15 "Zekes" approaching and attacked it, claiming ten shot down. 2Lt Malcolm Birney was lost to one of the "Zekes," however.

Immediately after this combat Valentine observed what he identified as three "Tojos" and three "Vals" (Type 99 Carrier Bombers). It is more likely, given the units involved that morning, that this was a formation of "Franks" escorting several Type 97 Fighters

The pilots of VMF-323 sit on the wing of one of the squadron's Corsairs on Okinawa. VMF-323 claimed seven "Tojos" shot down on May 25, 1945, but these were more likely to have been Ki-84 "Franks" from several Shimbu-Tai units that sortied that day with their Ki-84 escorts. (Jack Lambert Collection, Museum of Flight)

or Type 2 Advanced Trainers (Ki-79s), both of which were active that day – the latter machines also had fixed undercarriages like the "Val." Valentine initially climbed and then dived on the formation, shooting down two of the "Tojos" with hits in the engine and the cockpit – his wingman Lt William Farrell dispatched the third fighter. Valentine also claimed two "Vals" shot down for his fifth and sixth kills of the day.

Shortly thereafter VMF-322 engaged another Japanese formation, claiming seven "Tojos" shot down – 2Lt James Webster was credited with three kills and a fourth as a probable. A division from VMF-323 was next, attacking a formation the division identified as seven "Tojos," one "Tony" and two "Zekes" flying in loose formation, noticing that two of the "Tojos" were carrying bombs. 1Lt John Strickland claimed a "Tojo" and a "Zeke," while 1Lts Charles Allen and James Feliton were credited with two "Tojos" each, 2Lt Thomas Blackwell claiming the sixth. Some 30 miles away, 2Lt Stuart Alley claimed another "Tojo" shot down following an intense duel.

On May 28, during Kikusui Operation No 8, a division from VF-85 came across four Ki-84s flying in formation. These may have been from the 58th and 59th Shimbu-Tai, which sent out four Hayates that day. Lieutenant (jg) Kennard Moos, flying an F4U-1D, claimed two "Franks" shot down, while Lt(jg)s James Egolf and David Lawhon claimed one each flying cannon-armed F4U-1Cs.

Despite the Ki-84 units suffering terribly at the hands of US fighters, there were several combats during this period that show the capabilities of the Hayate to advantage. On May 4, Maj Michiaki Tojo, commanding the 103rd Hikō Sentai, led a formation of Hayates from his own unit and the 102nd Hikō Sentai that were charged with escorting a mixed Special Attack airplane formation consisting of Ki-27 "Nates," Ki-43 "Oscars," Ki-84 "Franks" and two Ki-45 "Nicks" (Type 2 Two-seat Fighters) to Okinawa. More "Oscars" from the 65th Hikō Sentai also participated in the mission.

That same morning VF-85 sent up three divisions on CAP north of Okinawa. Flying at 20,000ft, Ens E. L. Myers, wingman to Lt(jg) Saul Chernoff, saw a formation of what he identified as 12-16 "Zekes," and Chernoff ordered him to take the lead. The other members of the division found that the 20mm cannon in their F4U-1Cs had frozen and had to break off the attack. Chernoff continued, seeing that the Japanese

1. Armored glass
2. Mk 8 reflector gunsight
3. Gun switch box
4. Bomb switch box
5. Water injection quantity warning light
6. Stall warning light
7. Carburetor air temperature warning light
8. Engine speed indicator
9. Auxiliary drop tank fuel control switch
10. Altimeter
11. Manifold pressure gauge
12. Directional gyro
13. Airspeed indicator
14. Compass
15. Turn and bank indicator
16. Artificial horizon
17. Rate of climb/descent indicator
18. Elapsed time clock
19. Cylinder temperature indicator
20. Oil temperature indicator
21. Oil pressure gauge
22. Fuel pressure gauge
23. Instrument panel lights
24. Flap control/indicator
25. Ignition switch
26. Alternate air control
27. Throttle lever
28. Supercharger control
29. Landing gear and dive brake control lever
30. Gun charging control
31. Mixture control lever
32. Propeller control lever
33. Aileron trimming tab control wheel/indicator
34. Fuel tank selector
35. Hydraulic hand pump
36. Elevator trimming tab control wheel
37. Elevator trimming tab indicator
38. Rudder trimming tab control wheel/indicator
39. Tail wheel locking handle
40. Rudder pedals
41. Control grip with gun-firing button
42. Control column
43. Cockpit ventilator
44. Signal pistol cartridge container
45. Rocket station distributor box
46. Main tank fuel contents gauge
47. Hydraulic pressure gauge
48. Voltmeter
49. Fuel tank pressure gauge
50. Accelerometer
51. Radio control box
52. Cooling flap control levers
53. Pilot's distribution box
54. Map case
55. Pilot's seat
56. Pilot's seat adjustment lever
57. Gunsight reflector glass

Ki-84 COCKPIT

1. Wing-mounted Ho-5 20mm cannon arming cock
2. Exhaust temperature gauge
3. Cylinder temperature gauge
4. Overboost control lever
5. Model 1 ignition switch
6. Landing gear position indicator
7. Propeller speed control
8. Type 1 oil temperature gauge
9. Type 100 tachometer
10. Type 2 boost pressure gauge
11. Type 3 speed indicator
12. Type 98 compass
13. Type 98 turn indicator
14. Artificial horizon cock
15. Type 98 artificial horizon
16. Cockpit airflow control lever
17. Army Type 3 reflecting gunsight
18. Main instrument panel

19. Type 97 vertical speed indicator
20. Type 97 altimeter
21. Type 100 aeronautic clock
22. Oxygen flow gauge
23. Type 95 fuel gauge
24. Data table
25. Type 1 fuel gauge
26. Two-speed compressor oil pressure gauge
27. Tank pressurization fuel pressure gauge
28. Turn indicator adjustment
29. Oil gauge selector
30. Airspeed indicator rain remover
31. Tank pressurization selector
32. Electric box
33. Type 95 oil gauge
34. Ho-103 12.7mm machine gun loading cock

35. Rudder peddle position adjustment handle
36. "Hi" Mk 3 wireless receiver
37. Type 94 oil pressure gauge
38. Rudder pedals
39. Ultraviolet cockpit light
40. Cannon firing switch
41. Main power switch
42. Starter switch
43. Oil cooler shutter control
44. Cowl flap control lever
45. Seat light
46. Dust filter control lever
47. Air warmer control lever
48. Five-way cock control lever
49. Manual oil pressure pump lever
50. Control column
51. Three-way cock control lever
52. Seat
53. Elevator trim tab control

54. Canopy open lever
55. Throttle lever
56. Manual propeller pitch control lever
57. Radio remote control
58. Supercharger zero-speed selector lever
59. Supercharger automatic high-altitude valve selector lever
60. Supercharger two-speed selector lever
61. High altitude valve adjustment lever
62. Flap control
63. Landing gear control
64. Tail wheel lock control
65. Ho-103 12.7mm machine guns
66. Seat height adjustment lever

65

aircraft were in two formations, one higher and one lower. He decided to attack the higher formation on his own in order to protect Ens Myers, even though he would be attacking from below. Another division of VF-85 was climbing rapidly to help.

Chernoff came in on what he identified as a formation of "Zekes" and opened fire with his cannon, knocking the port wing off one airplane. He fired on a second, which blew up under his fire, then came down to make a run on two more fighters, firing three bursts at one that blew up (these may well have been "Franks," as the 60th Shinbu-Tai lost three that day and the escort force lost eight). As he tried, and failed, to follow the second fighter through a turn, Chernoff noticed three "Zekes" coming down on him from above.

Maj Tojo had been watching the Special Attack airplanes targeting what he thought was a group of US Navy cruisers and destroyers when he saw two Corsairs come into view below him, one behind the other. They were firing on the Special Attack airplanes, and apparently did not see him. The second Corsair, apparently flown by Lt(jg) F. S. Siddell, came within range and Tojo immediately opened fire and sent it down smoking. Chernoff did not see Tojo closing behind him, the Ki-84 pilot opening fire and hitting the Corsair's engine, which began to smoke badly and covered the windscreen with oil. Chernoff did a split-S to escape, but his Corsair was finished. Major Tojo was not sure how badly he had damaged the two Corsairs, but wisely did not follow them down. Chernoff and Siddell were badly hit, but both made water landings and were rescued. With an experienced pilot at the controls and an altitude advantage, the Hayate had shot down two Corsairs in under a minute.

2Lt Stuart Alley had the good fortune to survive a combat with an experienced Japanese fighter pilot during this same encounter, as VMF-323's Aircraft Action Report recorded:

> Lt Alley, at 500ft, sighted a single Tojo flying in the opposite direction at 4000ft. When sighted the Tojo was making a run on Lt Alley from above at 11 o'clock, Lt Alley pulling up his nose and firing back at the approaching Tojo. A burst or two

A VF-85 Corsair attacks a "Frank" during the combat of May 28, 1945. VF-85 pilots claimed four Ki-84s shot down this day, two with the F4U-1D and two with the cannon-armed F4U-1C. (RG38, VF-85 Aircraft Action Report for May 28, 1945, NARA)

was exchanged and Lt Alley noticed the Tojo's engine slightly smoking and pieces flying off the Tojo's fuselage. Both overshot the termination of this first pass, and both then scrambled to get altitude advantage. Lt Alley managed to get above the Tojo and initiated his second pass from above at 12 o'clock. A few scattered hits were noticed, hitting around the Tojo's engine cowling, before Lt Alley passed by the Tojo on this run. Lt Alley recovered fast and again got an altitude advantage. A third pass was then made slightly above at 6 o'clock. Lt Alley opened fire at 350 yards and closed fast. The Tojo jinked violently but was smoking badly. The Tojo dove for the water, crashed and exploded.

2Lt Stuart Alley of VMF-323, who encountered an experienced and determined Japanese fighter pilot during the May 25 combats around Okinawa and fortunately came out the winner of the duel. (RG 127, 127-GW-123083, NARA)

Commenting on comparative performance between the "Tojo" (almost certainly one of the escorting Hayate fighters from the 102nd or 103rd Hikō Sentai), the report said, "The Tojo Lt Alley destroyed was very aggressive, and very fast. The pilot displayed excellent airmanship – the Tojo proved to be an equal match for the Corsair in both dives and turns."

One of the last encounters between the Corsair and the Hayate occurred during Kikusui Operation No 10. This was the first combat with a "Frank" involving the latest model of the Corsair, the F4U-4, which had significantly better performance. On that day, June 21, 1Lt Martin Tiernan was leading a division from VMF-223 on a barrier CAP over the islands north of Okinawa. VMF-223 had arrived on Okinawa earlier in the month, missing out on the intense air combat of April and May. By June, the JAAF and IJNAF were running out of Special Attack pilots. For this last Kikusui attack the JAAF sent out just 15 Special Attack aircraft over two days and the IJNAF only 30. On the first day of the attack the 26th Shimbu-Tai unit sent out four Ki-84s to attack shipping west of Okinawa, apparently with an escort force.

Flying at 10,000ft in the late afternoon, Tiernan was following a vector from the Fighter Director when he spotted a formation of 12 aircraft flying abreast at 8,000ft, with two divisions in the middle and a section of two aircraft on either end. In the fading light Tiernan thought they were P-47s, but as the division closed in he identified them as "Tojos." Tiernan and his wingman, 1Lt John Groot, took on the section on the right, while his element leader, 1Lt Arthur Evans, took the section on the left. Tiernan closed to within 50 yards of the Japanese wingman and apparently killed the pilot with a burst into the cockpit. Turning to take on the leader, he saw tracers going past his right wing – the Japanese pilot had apparently seen the attack and reacted with speed and maneuverability to whip around and come in on Tiernan's Corsair. Fortunately, Tiernan's wingman was in position to fire on the attacking fighter, sending it down smoking. Evans and his wingman, 2Lt Roy McAlister Jr, shot down the two aircraft in the other section on the left of the

F4U-1C and F4U-1D Corsairs onboard USS *Shangri-La* (CV-38), with the Royal Australian Navy destroyer HMAS *Napier* (D15) keeping station alongside the carrier. VF-85 and VBF-85 used these Corsairs interchangeably, flying missions using both models in the same division. (RG-80, 80-G-278801, NARA)

formation. While this combat was going on, the remaining eight aircraft used their speed to reach a cloud layer and escape.

On this date the 47th Hikō Sentai lost a Type 4 Fighter over Okinawa, and since these were the only aircraft claimed that day in that area, it seems probable that the "Tojos" VMF-223 ran into were "Franks" from the 26th Shimbu-Tai unit, with an escort from the 47th Hikō Sentai. This unit had been transferred to Kyushu on May 27 to defend the Kyushu airfields and to provide escorts to the Special Attack units. It was a quick and one-sided encounter, giving evidence of the F4U-4's superiority. As VMF-223's Aircraft Action Report stated, "the enemy airplanes were outclassed by the F4U-4s, which closed on them from above and showed superior speed."

The next day the 27th Shimbu-Tai and the 179th Shimbu-Tai sent out 11 Type 4 Special Attack aircraft to attack American vessels west of Okinawa. That morning 2Lt Duncan Urquhart with VMF-322 claimed a "Tojo" southwest of Okinawa, which may have been one of the "Franks" from the Shimbu-Tai units.

The last combat between the Corsair and the "Frank" almost certainly took place on July 25, 1945, and it proved to be an uneven contest. Early that morning ten Corsairs from VF-85, consisting of eight F4U-1Cs and two F4U-1Ds, joined 12 F6F-5s from VF-88 on a fighter sweep over the Japanese airfields of Miho and Yonaga, on the southwest coast of Honshu. The Corsairs of VF-85 struck Yonaga while VF-88 attacked Miho, dropping 260lb fragmentation bombs and firing 5in. rockets. Coming in on a strafing run Ens Loyd Miller caught a Japanese fighter he identified as a "Frank" just as it was taking off. A burst from the four 20mm cannon in Miller's F4U-1C hit the Ki-84 in the engine, sending it crashing near the airfield.

In the final weeks of the Pacific War neither US Navy nor US Marine Corps Corsair squadrons appear to have met "Franks" in the few remaining clashes fought over Japan.

STATISTICS AND ANALYSIS

The aerial engagements between the Corsair and the Hayate took place from February to July 1945. The two fighters met in combat perhaps 20 times, taking into account the confusion over aircraft recognition in the heat of battle and the lack of available JAAF records. Since many of these combats appear to have involved Corsairs attacking Ki-84s from the Shimbu-Tai Special Attack units that were flown by less-experienced pilots, it can be argued that these actions are not representative of the capabilities of the Hayate versus the Corsair. But even if the superior performance of the Ki-84 improved the odds for all pilots regardless of their level of experience, the introduction of the Type 4 fighter in the defense of Japan did little to alter the outcome of the battle.

In the duels between the Corsair and the Hayate, the F4U won handily, although it was not without effort. Fortunately for the US Navy and US Marine Corps Corsair pilots the Hayates were too few in number with too few experienced pilots to alter the outcome significantly of the aerial battles waged against superior numbers of American fighter airplanes flown by better-trained pilots.

Determining the number of Corsairs that fell to the Type 4 and the number of Type 4s that fell to the Corsair with any degree of precision is an exercise in frustration because of the problems of aircraft recognition and the paucity of information currently available from the Japanese side. After World War II, the US Navy published *Naval Aviation Combat Statistics – World War II*, which gives a listing of claims against different types of Japanese aircraft from September 1, 1944 to August 15, 1945. This report states that US Navy and US Marine Corps Corsairs shot down 28 "Franks" during this period, but also 53 "Tojos" and seven "Georges."

Although this VBF-85 Corsair was damaged in a combat with the N1K2-J "George," this photograph illustrates the destructive power of the 20mm cannon that equipped JAAF late-war fighters like the Ki-84 and the Ki-100. (RG38, VBF-85 Aircraft Action Report for June 2, 1945, NARA)

The historical information available today indicates that several encounters between what US Navy and US Marine Corps pilots identified as "Franks" were actually combats with "Georges" from the IJNAF's 343rd Kokutai, while many of the claims for "Tojos" were in all likelihood actually the "Franks" of the Shimbu-Tai units and their escorts. If one looks at the combats during the period in which the US Navy or US Marine Corps pilots specifically claimed "Franks" (excluding the combats that can be attributed to battles with the 343rd Kokutai), and adds the combats that took place during the Okinawa campaign and the Kikusui attacks in which US Navy and US Marine Corps Corsairs claimed "Tojos" that can be linked with the Shimbu-Tai units flying the Type 4 (admittedly, a somewhat subjective exercise), one comes up with the total of approximately 67 fighters shot down that were probably, but not certainly, Type 4 fighters.

Corsair losses to the Hayate are equally difficult to attribute with any degree of certainty, particularly in the absence of Japanese records of claims against the American fighter. As the US Navy's statistical study commented, "the errors in identification which may normally be expected in the action reports results in a decrease of accuracy which leaves something to be desired, but permits comparisons which are believed to be sufficiently near the truth to be of considerable value and interest, and are in any event the best available." The US Navy listed four Corsairs lost against claims for "Franks," and four lost against claims for "Tojos." In addition, the US Navy listed three losses to "Jacks" and, oddly, no losses to the "George."

When comparing claims to losses, the US Navy added one unidentified loss of a Corsair to losses against the "Frank," "Jack" and "George." The US Navy reported a ratio of six late-war Japanese fighters ("Frank," "Jack" and "George") destroyed for each Corsair lost. Adding in claims for "Tojos" that may have been "Franks" takes the ratio up to

around seven-to-one, giving the Corsair a clear superiority. But this contrasts with the Corsair's twelve-to-one record against the "Zeke" during this period, clearly indicating that the more capable Japanese fighters were in fact more difficult to shoot down.

For the US Navy and US Marine Corps Corsair pilots, the "Frank" was just one of many Japanese fighters they encountered in aerial battles over Kyushu and Okinawa. They were far more likely to encounter the "Zeke." Given the intensity of the fighting over Okinawa and the relatively few encounters between the Corsair and the "Frank," spread over three US Navy and nine US Marine Corsair squadrons, not to mention the positive outcome of almost all of these combats, it is not surprising that the Ki-84 did not make a dramatic impression.

It is possible, however, to detect a degree of respect for the Japanese fighter from comments in the Aircraft Action Reports. These remarks relate to speed, maneuverability and protection. Some reports, but not all, noted that the "Frank" was nearly as fast as the Corsair. On a mission to Kyushu on May 14, the Corsairs of VMF-112 ran into a formation of Hayates from the 100th Hikōshidan flying a patrol and went in pursuit. As the Aircraft Action Report noted:

> This was the first time the Corsairs had battled a number of the new Jap Franks. When the Franks were first sighted they were approximately three miles away in a slight dive. The Corsairs started after them from level flight. The leading Franks were able to maintain their distance advantage, but the Corsairs did manage to close on the last three Franks. It was evident from this performance that the Franks had every bit as much speed as the Corsairs although Maj Andre thought in a prolonged chase the Corsair might catch the Frank.

After fighting with Ki-84s during a CAP on May 28, the pilots of VF-85 commented that the "Frank" was "more maneuverable than the F4U-1C" and "could easily turn inside it." From the same combat, VF-85 pilots added that the "'Frank' had very good protection. After being hit in the wings it burned a very short while then

The Ki-84 was the most numerous JAAF fighter airplane in the final months of the war, with 353 serving in the Home Islands, Korea, Manchuria, China and Formosa in August 1945. These Ki-84s were assigned to the 104th Hikō Sentai in Korea at the end of the war. Note the lone Ki-36 "Ida" army cooperation airplane behind the closest "Frank." (Courtesy Philip Jarrett)

The JAAF developed its own gunsights separately from the IJNAF. Most Ki-84s used the Army Type 3 gunsight, a replacement for the earlier Type 100 reflector gunsight. The Type 3 was based on the German Revi 12C gunsight and featured a larger reticule than the Type 100.

The Ki-84's mixed armament of Ho-103 12.7mm machine guns and Ho-5 20mm cannon presented its pilots with a mix of trajectories, but the two weapons had the benefit of similar rates of fire and muzzle velocities. The Ho-103 round had a muzzle velocity of 760 meters a second, while the Ho-5 round traveled 700 meters in a second. The Ho-103 put out 15 rounds a second, while the Ho-5 could fire off 14 rounds. The Ho-103's 12.7mm round was similar in effect to the American 0.50in round, but the 20mm round of the Ho-5

had nearly double the destructive power. The projectile weight of the Ho-5's 20mm round was three times heavier than the 12.7mm round of the Ho-103 machine gun. A few rounds could do significant damage to a Corsair. There were several examples where an F4U that made it back to the carrier after receiving 20mm hits in the wing had to have the latter entirely replaced. It was fortunate for American pilots that Nakajima produced only limited numbers of the Ki-84 Otsu (Ki-84b) armed with four Ho-5 cannon.

Once again, pilot experience was a factor. Most Japanese pilots at this stage of the war had only limited experience with aerial gunnery. Knocking down a Corsair required hits in a vital area such as the engine – not an easy target for a beginner in fast-moving combat.

smoked slightly. Very hard to explode." Other squadrons had similar experiences, VMF-221 noting that "armour appears to be definitely present, as none burned and all hit many times."

Summarizing the experiences of VF-84 against the "Frank" and the "George." Lt Cdr Roger Hedrick probably reflected the views of most US Navy and US Marine Corps pilots who encountered these fighters when he stated that "the F4U-1D was found to be superior to the latest Jap models. The edge over the Frank and the George is not large but is ample to gain victory by aggressive attack." But in so many combats, the level of pilot experience was the most telling factor. The comments of VMF-441 on this score are representative:

> In each case the enemy pilots appeared to ours to be inexperienced and not aggressive. None of the enemy aircraft fired on our planes and they did not take advantage of their superior maneuverability.

Pilot experience appears to have been the Achilles heel of the Type 4 Fighter Sentai in the final battles of the Pacific War. With its superior flying characteristics and performance over the Type 1 and Type 2 fighters, the Hayate was well-liked by JAAF fighter pilots, and as one aviator who survived the war said, "I'm sure there's no need for me to comment on the advantages of its high speed and Ho-5 20mm cannon." While the Type 4 was easier for the young pilots coming out of training in 1944 and 1945 to adjust to, it is not surprising that it was the more experienced pilots who were able to take advantage of the Hayate's performance.

Among the more successful Ki-84 pilots in the final months of the war was WO Katsuki Kira, who scored nine victories during the battles over the Nomonhan, claimed seven more over New Guinea, several in the Philippines and achieved the last of his 21 victories fighting over Okinawa with the 103rd Hikō Sentai. Maj Hyoe

The F4U-4 made its combat debut in June 1945 with the Corsair squadrons of MAG-14 on Okinawa and with VBF-6 onboard USS *Hancock* (CV-19) and VBF-94 onboard USS *Lexington* (CV-16). (US Marine Corps Museum)

Yonaga was another Nomonhan veteran who fought in the Okinawa battles as commander of the 101st Hikō Sentai, ending the war with 16 victory claims. As described earlier, Maj Michiaki Tojo, another experienced pilot, shot down two Corsairs in the Okinawa battles. It is also important to note that three pilots from the 103rd Hikō Sentai, Capt Tomojiro Ogawa and 1Lts Yasushi Miyamotobayashi and Shigeyasu Miyamoto, were all awarded the *Bukōshō* medal, Japan's highest award for gallantry for their actions during the Okinawa air battles. But there were far too few pilots of this caliber to make a difference in these final battles, particularly against American numerical superiority.

Maj Tojo's experience following his combat with Navy Corsairs on May 4 is perhaps representative of the frustrations many of the JAAF's fighter pilots felt at the time. In a postwar interview he recalled what happened as he led his formation of Hayate fighters back to base:

> On our way home we took the course on the island's line [following the Ryukyu Island chain back to Kyushu]. When we flew at an altitude of 4000m west of Yaku-shima, I saw some hundreds of enemy carrier-based planes flying at an altitude of 3000m in tight formations like a military review. There were also fighter squadrons in fighting formation above them, flying grandly back to the south. I thought the possibility if our 30 planes could attack them from behind, but I decided no, "We have many young birds [with] less than 300 hours. I should be patient." We continued to fly north. I thought the enemies were the same. Both didn't want a fight. The situation was greatly different from that when we had combats in the south years earlier. Skills of fighter pilots [had gone] down.

Corsair Pilots' "Frank" Victory Claims			
Pilot	**Unit**	**Claims**	**Date**
Ens Roy Rechsteiner	VBF-83	2 "Franks"	April 5, 1945
Lt(jg) Cyrus Chambers	VF-84	2 "Franks"	April 28, 1945
Lt Cdr Roger Hedrick	VF-84	2 "Franks"	February 2, 1945
Lt(jg) Kennard Moos	VF-85	2 "Franks"	May 28, 1945
2Lt Wendell Browning	VMF-112	1.5 "Franks"*	April 14, 1945
Capt William Snider	VMF-221	2 "Franks"	March 18, 1945
2Lt Raymond Barrett	VMF-311	2 "Franks"	June 8, 1945
Capt Herbert Valentine	VMF-312	2 "Franks"*	May 25, 1945
2Lt Jay Allen	VMF-322	1.5 "Franks"*	May 25, 1945
2Lt James Webster	VMF-322	3 "Franks"*	May 25, 1945
1Lt Charles Allen	VMF-323	2 "Franks"*	May 25, 1945
1Lt James Feliton	VMF-323	2 "Franks"*	May 25, 1945
* These were claimed as "Tojos" during the Kikusui attacks			

AFTERMATH

Following the fall of Okinawa, the JAAF ordered all of its air units to conserve their strength for the expected invasion of the Home Islands – they were not to respond to American raids. It lifted this restriction when it realized that American bomber and fighter attacks were severely disrupting aircraft production. The order does explain the dearth of combats between the Corsair and the Hayate following the loss of Okinawa. Towards the end of the campaign the 6th Kōkūgun had been returned to Army control. The General Air Army, formed in April to command and control all JAAF air units in the Home Islands, now commanded the 1st Kōkūgun and the 6th Kōkūgun. Together these two formations had eight Sentai equipped with the Type 4 Fighter covering Honshu, Shikoku and Kyushu. Serviceability was a problem. At the end of

The Tachikawa Aircraft Company undertook the development of a wooden version of the Type 4 Fighter to conserve resources. Designated the Ki-106, this effort did not go beyond a few prototypes. (Peter M. Bowers Collection, Museum of Flight)

In the last few months of the
Pacific War the US Navy converted
more Corsair squadrons to the
F4U-4, particularly the fighter-
bomber units. These examples
were assigned to VBF-89 onboard
USS *Antietam* (CV-36) in July
1945. (RG80, 80-G-333509)

the war the JAAF reported to Allied authorities that there were 267 Type 4 Fighters in Japan, but only 162 were operational.

Production, or lack of it, was also a continuing problem. With the Type 4 Fighter, it peaked in December 1944 at 373 airplanes, and declined thereafter. In July Nakajima built 184 Type 4 Fighters at its two plants, but as previously mentioned production of the Ha-45 Homare engine lagged behind aircraft construction. The bombing of Nakajima's aircraft factories, the move to start production in dispersed underground facilities and the impact of raids on urban areas around the factories reduced productivity. Production of the Type 4 at the Mansyu Hikoki Seizo K.K. (Manchurian Airplane Manufacturing Co Ltd) factory in Manchuria had begun in early 1945, but less than 100 airplanes were built.

To conserve diminishing supplies of critical aluminium, the Tachikawa Hikoki K.K. (Tachikawa Aircraft Company) undertook the design and development of an all-wood version of the Type 4 as the Ki-106. Three prototypes were built and were under test when the war ended. Nakajima worked on a Ki-84 built with carbon steel components and sheeting (as the Ki-113), but this proved to be significantly overweight. Even if Nakajima had been able to increase production of the Hayate, there was insufficient fuel for major operations, and pilot training had been limited almost exclusively to training pilots for Special Attack missions. Given all the constraints on resources, it is doubtful that the JAAF could have overcome the problem of inexperienced pilots.

There were several advanced designs of the Ki-84 undertaken at Nakajima during the last year of the war, drawing on the company's experience with the Ki-87 experimental high altitude fighter. These were intended as interceptors to combat the B-29s. The first was the Ki-84-III, which simply replaced the Ha-45 Homare with the Ha-44 12Ru engine of 2,450hp and added a turbo-supercharger under the fuselage. This airplane did not progress beyond the design stage. The Ki-84R exchanged the turbo-supercharger for a mechanically driven device and incorporated a wing of larger area. More ambitious designs were the Ki-84N and the Ki-84P, featuring the Ha-44-13Ru engine giving 2,500hp, a turbo-supercharger and increased wing area. The Kōkū Hombu decided to pursue the Ki-84N and assigned it the designation Ki-117, but this, too, remained only a design.

Vought undertook no further development of the Corsair during World War II, concentrating on production. It stopped building the F4U-1D in February 1945, switching to production of the more capable F4U-4. By the end of the Pacific War Vought had completed 1,850 F4U-4s, compared to 1,485 Type 4 fighters built during the same period. Goodyear Aircraft undertook development of the F2G-1 Corsair, using the Pratt & Whitney R4360 Wasp Major giving 3,000hp. Although the F2G-1 had a terrific rate of climb, its performance was not sufficiently greater than the F4U-4 or the newer F8F-1 then coming into service. The Bureau of Aeronautics canceled the F2G-1 production order in May 1945.

By early August 1945, the US Navy had 11 squadrons of F4U-4s with the Fast Carrier Task Force either in the Pacific or preparing for combat on the West Coast. Ten of these were fighter-bomber squadrons, as the Corsair had proved to be more capable in this role than the Hellcat. MAG-14 remained the only Marine Air Group on Okinawa with the F4U-4, the other US Marine Corps squadrons retaining the F4U-1D/FG-1D/F4U-1C. Had the war continued, it is likely that more "Marine Air" Corsair squadrons would have converted to the F4U-4, as Vought had contracts for an additional 3,900 that were canceled after the end of the war.

FURTHER READING

Akimoto, Minoru, Ikari, Yoshio et al, *Yon-Shiki Sentoki Hayate (Nakajima Army Type 4 Fighter Hayate (Ki-84))*, *The Maru Mechanic No 33* (Ushio Shobo, 1982)

Brown, Capt Eric 'Winkle', RN, *Wings of the Navy – Testing British and US Carrier Aircraft*. Revised Edition (Hikoki Publications, 2013)

Cea, Eduardo, *Japanese Military Aircraft No 8: Tokubetsu Kogeki Tai. Special Attack Units* (AF Editions, 2011)

Condon, John Pomeroy, *Corsairs and Flatops – Marine Carrier Air Warfare 1944–1945* (Naval Institute Press, 1998)

Dean, Francis H., *America's Hundred-Thousand – US Production Fighters of World War 2* (Schiffer, 1997)

Ferkl, Martin, *Nakajima Ki-44 Shoki* (Revi, 2009)

Green, William and Swanborough, Gordon, *World War II Fact Files – Japanese Army Fighters, Part 2* (Macdonald and Janes, 1977)

Guyton, Boone T., *Whispering Death – The Test Pilot's Story of the F4U Corsair* (Orion Books, 1990)

Harvey, Ralph, *Developing the Gull-Winged F4U Corsair And Taking It To Sea* (Privately published, 2012)

Hata, Ikuhiko, Izawa, Yasuho and Shores, Christopher, *Japanese Army Air Force Fighter Units and Their Aces 1931–1945* (Grub Street, 2002)

Ikari, Yoshiro, *Sentoki Hayate (Hayate Fighter)* (Shirogane Shobo, 1976)

Japanese Monograph No 157, *Homeland Air Defense Operations Record* (Office of the Chief of Military History, 1952)

Model Art No 451, *Special Issue – Imperial Japanese Army Air Force Suicide Attack Unit* (Model Art Co, 1995)

Nohara, Shigaru et al, *Hayate Rikugun Yon-Shiki Sentoki (Hayate Army Type 4 Fighter Ki-84)* (Model Art No 283, 1986)

Nohara, Shigaru et al, *Nakajima Rikugun Yon-Shiki Sentoki Hayate (Ki-84) (Nakajima Army Type 4 Fighter Hayate (Ki-84)* (Model Art 493, 1997)

O'Brien, Phillips Payson, *How the War Was Won – Air-Sea Power and Allied Victory in World War II* (Cambridge University Press, 2015)

Rielly, Robin L., *Kamikaze Attacks of World War II – A Complete History of Japanese Suicide Strikes on American Ships, by Aircraft and Other Means* (McFarland & Co, 2010)

Sakaida, Henry, Osprey Aircraft of the Aces 13 – *Japanese Army Air Force Aces 1937–45* (Osprey Publishing, 1997)

Sakaida, Henry and Takaki, Koji, *Genda's Blade – Japan's Squadron of Aces – 343rd Kokutai* (Classic Publications, 2003)

Szlagor, Tomasz and Wieliczko, Leszek A., *Kagero Monographs No 52 – Vought F4U Corsair, Vol. I* (Kagero, 2013)

Szlagor, Tomasz and Wieliczko, Leszek A., *Kagero Monographs No 56 – Vought F4U Corsair, Vol. II* (Kagero, 2014)

Tillman, Barrett, *Corsair – The F4U in World War II and Korea* (Naval Institute Press, 1979)

Tokkotai Senbotsusha Irei Heiwa Kinen Kyokai, Interview with Maj Michiaki Tojo (Tokko, 2004) available at: http://cs.iupui.edu/~ateal/Ingraham/May4/Tojo.html (Last accessed 18 November 2015)

Watanabe, Yoji, *Kessen no So-ku-e – Nihon Sentoki Retuden (To the Blue Skies of Decisive Battles – Japanese Fighter Plane Biographies)* (Privately published, 2010)

Wieliczko, Leszek A., *Kagero Monographs No 53 – Nakajima Ki-84 Hayate* (Kagero, 2013)

Yon-Shiki Sentoki Hayate (Pacific War No 46) (Bunshan Bunko, 2004)

INDEX